Texts from Jane Eyre

Texts from Jane Eyre

And Other Conversations with Your Favourite Literary Characters

Mallory Ortberg

corsair

CORSAIR

First published in the United States of America in 2014 by
Henry Holt and Company, LLC

First published in Great Britain in 2015 by Corsair

1 3 5 7 9 10 8 6 4 2

A CIP catalogue record for this book
is available from the British Library.

ISBN: 978-1-472150-73-8 (hardback)
ISBN: 978-1-472150-74-5 (ebook)

Printed and bound by CPI Group (UK) Ltd, Croydon, CR0 4YY

Papers used by Corsair are from well-managed forests
and other responsible sources.

MIX
Paper from
responsible sources
FSC www.fsc.org FSC® C104740

Corsair
An imprint of
Little, Brown Book Group
Carmelite House
50 Victoria Embankment
London EC4Y 0DZ

An Hachette UK Company
www.hachette.co.uk

www.littlebrown.co.uk

Contents

Part II

Part III

Part IV

Texts from Jane Eyre

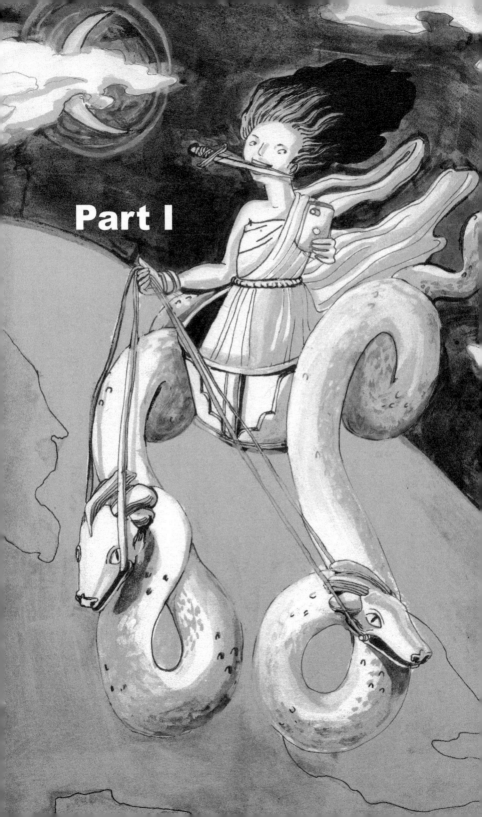

Part I

Medea

hiiiiiiii

hi who is this

it's Glauce right??
that is such a pretty name
I am so crazy about how pretty your name is
"Jason and Glauce" sounds so good together

thank you
who is this?

when is the WEDDING
I hope you guys have the Argonauts as groomsmen
and they do the sword thing
you know where they make the little roof with their swords
and you run down underneath it
it's so cute
oh my god what am I saying
you probably already have a million plans, it's your wedding
it was just my favorite part of my wedding
(except for the part where I married Jason!!!)
(he is so fun to be married to)
(tell him I say hi!!!)

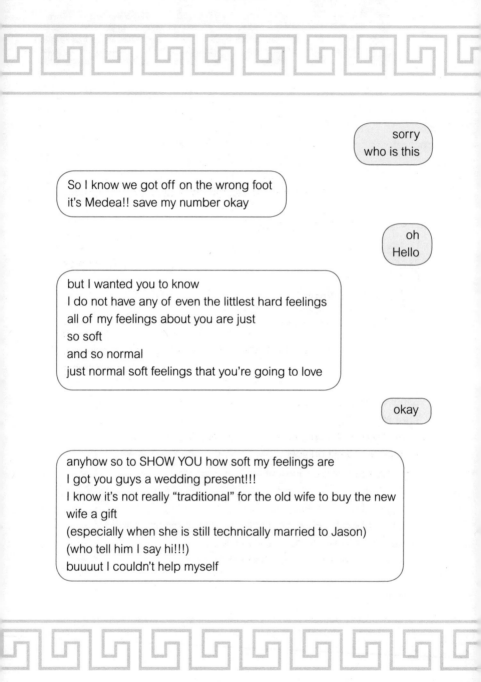

> sorry
> who is this

So I know we got off on the wrong foot
it's Medea!! save my number okay

> oh
> Hello

but I wanted you to know
I do not have any of even the littlest hard feelings
all of my feelings about you are just
so soft
and so normal
just normal soft feelings that you're going to love

> okay

anyhow so to SHOW YOU how soft my feelings are
I got you guys a wedding present!!!
I know it's not really "traditional" for the old wife to buy the new wife a gift
(especially when she is still technically married to Jason)
(who tell him I say hi!!!)
buuuut I couldn't help myself

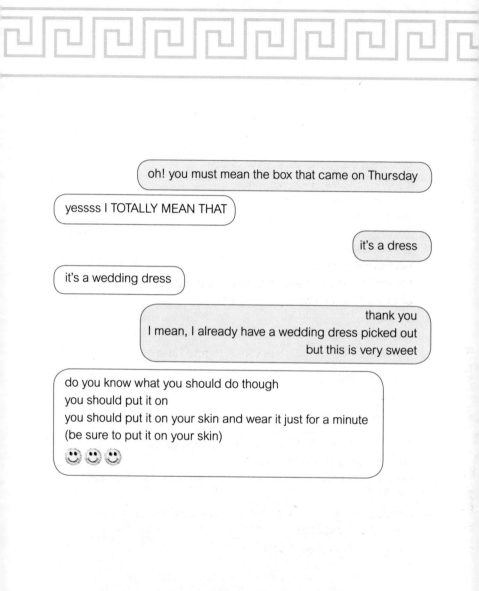

oh! you must mean the box that came on Thursday

yessss I TOTALLY MEAN THAT

it's a dress

it's a wedding dress

thank you
I mean, I already have a wedding dress picked out
but this is very sweet

do you know what you should do though
you should put it on
you should put it on your skin and wear it just for a minute
(be sure to put it on your skin)

Gilgamesh

come along Gilgamesh
be you my husband
to me grant your lusciousness
I will harness for you a chariot of lapis lazuli
with wheels of gold
be my husband and I will be your wife

oh wow
Ishtar
that's so flattering
I'm so flattered

the Lullubu people will bring you produce of the mountains
as tribute
your she-goats will bear triplets

that's such a tempting offer

your ewes twins
your donkey will overtake the mule

i would just
love to
but super quick question
how is your boyfriend Tammuz
these days
is he still
trapped in the Underworld?

I don't know what you mean

how about all your other boyfriends
still horribly dead
or turned into wolves?

you know what
never mind

i'm just super curious
since you've murdered exactly all of them
if maybe you were planning
on doing that to me too

i hope you get eaten by dogs

there it is

Achilles

Achilles?
Kiddo? Achilles?
Hey bud you in there?
hey champ I know you're in there
I can see you
We just want to talk
okay?

no im not

you're not what
not in your tent?

no

buddy it's okay to be a little upset

IM NOT UPSET

okay

IM FULL OF RIGHTEOUS FURY

okay

THE ANGER OF ACHILLES SON OF PELEUS BRINGS
COUNTLESS ILL UPON THE ACHAEANS
SO I DONT GET "A LITTLE UPSET" OK

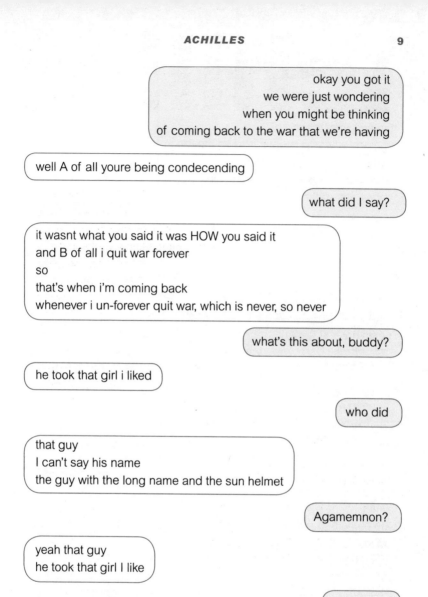

okay you got it
we were just wondering
when you might be thinking
of coming back to the war that we're having

well A of all youre being condecending

what did I say?

it wasnt what you said it was HOW you said it
and B of all i quit war forever
so
that's when i'm coming back
whenever i un-forever quit war, which is never, so never

what's this about, buddy?

he took that girl i liked

who did

that guy
I can't say his name
the guy with the long name and the sun helmet

Agamemnon?

yeah that guy
he took that girl I like

which girl?

I DONT REMEMBER
GOD
what is this
name remembering day
the one who was always holding the wine
or like the orb or whatever
she was always carrying something

okay
okay
would it help if we got her back?

no
it would not help
and youre being condescending again
and im going home

what will you do if you go home?

i dunno
stuff grows out of the ground if you put stuff in it
so maybe ill do that

farming?

yeah
go home and put stuff in the ground and no one will take the girls
i like
and i hope you all die in this stupid war

you don't mean that

you don't mean your face

what?

leave me alone

Dido

hey babe
when are you going to be home
tonight do you think

**This number has been disconnected
or is otherwise out of service.**

Plato

okay Glaucon so
i want you to picture a cave full of prisoners
who have been in the cave their whole lives
and they're all shackled in a line facing the back wall

my god
what a nightmare
those poor people

ok no
I mean yes, it's terrible, but no that's not the point
anyhow
they're shackled so they can only look at the back wall
they can't move their heads

what monster would do this

and there's a fire behind them

A FIRE IN THE CAVE
MY GOD
THESE POOR SOULS WILL BURN TO DEATH
WE MUST RESCUE THEM

no it's just
it's just a thought experiment
I want to talk about epistemology

WHAT FOUL SPIRIT WOULD CHAIN HUMAN BEINGS UNDER
THE EARTH LIKE HADES

no one
no one
they're just there

WE MUST MAKE HASTE
THESE SHACKLED CITIZENS CANNOT FREE THEMSELVES

it's an allegory
the cave is just an allegory

IMPOSSIBLE
IT IS THE WORK OF A KNAVE AND A BRIGAND
AND I SHALL NOT REST UNTIL HE IS DEAD

Circe

hi Odysseus
what are you doing for dinner tonight

Circe.

what
oh my god whatttt

Circe

stop it with my name
i don't know what you're mad about
are you mad

Circe I'm not coming over for dinner

whyyyyy

you know why

no I don't
I'm a witch
not a
not the captain of knowing why of things

what are all those pigs doing outside your house

I don't know
whatever pigs do
truffle-hunting

Circe

i think the technical term is mycophagy
but I'm not 100% on that

where did the pigs come from Circe

i don't know
a pig farm
a pig mommy and a pig daddy who loved each other very much
and gave each other a special handshake

CIRCE

oh my god okay fine
they're your crew, you got me
i turned all of your friends into pigs

why did you turn my friends into pigs

i don't know
maybe the real question is
why are your friends
so turn-into-pigsable

turn them back into humans

will you come over for dinner if i turn them back into humans

turn them back into humans first and we'll talk

uuugh
Finnnneeeee

and turn them back into REGULAR humans

what do you mean

just like how they were before
not
i don't know
half-pig men
or a thousand years old
or with no arms
just the same, normal people

haha oh my god
what do you even think i am
i would never do that

Circe
you own an entire island of badgermen

you don't know that island wasn't already like that when I got here

was it like
was it full of half-men half-badgers?

i don't have to answer that question
it was full of a lot of things when i got here
anyhow shut up
i fixed your stupid friends
who by the way are stupid and boring

CIRCE

im kiddddding godddd
🙂

Medea

hiiiiii
hi hi hi
its me again (Medea, just in case im not
already in your phone yet)
how was the dress???

> oh do you know
> I actually haven't had the chance to try it on yet
> I've been so busy

okay
okay that's not a problem
I sent you guys something else

> I don't think we have anything

look outside

> it's another box

THE BOX IS FROM ME
(are you surprised)

> a little bit
> how did you know where we live

i mean
how does anyone know anything right
you should open the box right now

The Wife of Bath

hey are you still up
can i come over

sure

its Allyson btw

cool

William Blake

hi

hi

I got you a present

you did?

I drew you something

oh wow
is it horrifying?

no

do you promise?
William?
do you promise me that it's not horrifying?

i drew you something

William
you know what I mean

what do you mean by horrifying

is anyone being
flayed alive in it
or committing suicide
or does something have eyes that shouldn't have eyes
you know what I mean
horrifying

never mind
sorry i bothered you

> William
> it isn't that
> you know I like your drawings

i know

> I just already have so many watercolors of flayings already
> I wouldn't know where to put another one

you could put it in the kitchen
you don't have hardly any of my flayings in there

> so it is a picture of someone being flayed

well
sort of
i mean they're already flayed but they're not getting flayed
it's not like a double flaying
ooh wait
hang on

■ ■ ■

Bring me my Bow of burning gold

> William what are you talking about

Bring me my Arrows of desire

> You're not allowed to have arrows
> has someone let you have arrows?

Bring me my Spear: O clouds unfold!

William
you don't have any of those things
and there aren't any clouds out
it's a very nice day
why don't you come outside in the garden for a little while
it's a very nice day out here

Bring me my Chariot of fire!

I can't do that, I'm afraid
but I can bring you a cup of tea
would you like me to bring you a cup of tea?
William?
would you like that?
it's no chariot of fire but I'll put lots of milk in it

bring me a cup of tea

I'll get you a cup of tea

a cup of tea of fire

what's that?

hmm?

what?

nothing
just a normal cup of tea with no fire in it yet
at all
not yet
ha ha ha ha ha

■ ■ ■

When the Sun rises do you not see a round Disk of fire
somewhat like a Guinea

I guess it could look like that

O no no I see an Innumerable company of the Heavenly host
oh
crying Holy Holy Holy is the Lord God Almighty

I guess it could be that too
either the money or the screaming angels

WOULD YOU QUESTION A WINDOW

what?

WOULD YOU QUESTION A WINDOW

I suppose not
I suppose I wouldn't

THEN NEITHER WILL I QUESTION MY CORPOREAL NOR VEGETATIVE EYE

■ ■ ■

Every thing in Dantes Comedia shews That for Tyrannical Purposes he has made This World the Foundation of All & the Goddess Nature & not the Holy Ghost

are you drawing pictures of Hell again

Keep just as you are – I will draw your portrait – for you have ever been an angel to me

okay
okay I'll keep real still
take all the time you want

what do you think would happen
if Heaven and Hell got MARRIED

I don't know

a Line or Lineament is not formed by Chance a Line is a Line in its Minutest Subdivision[s] Strait or Crooked It is Itself & Not Intermeasurable with or by any Thing Else Such is Job

are we
are we still talking about Hell
or are we talking about math now

King Lear

okay who wants a kingdom

me
me I do

how much do you love me

oh my god
how much DON'T I love you is a better question
i love you like i love eyes
or outer space
or standing up
or even this question
ahhhh that's so much haha

ahh that's so much

i knooooow

you can definitely have a kingdom

oh my god thank you
i hope you didn't think i was saying that
just to get a kingdom

oh no not at all

yayyyyyy

maybe after you take over i can come stay with you

oh
actually
that would not work for me
we're redoing a lot of the rooms right now
i'm so sorry!!!

hi babe :)
u coming over tonight

who is this

babe its regan
you know who i am

stop texting this number

wait who is this

leave me alone

edmund would never say that who is this
is this fucking goneril

no

it is
it totally is
you are so transparent
i can't believe you stole his phone

i didn't steal it
he's in the shower
if you must know

that's so pathetic

if it's so pathetic
then why is he here showering with me
instead of there
showering with you

obviously he isn't showering with you
obviously he's just showering
and you're alone
going through his phone
trying to make sure he doesn't get my messages

just leave him alone

i never let edmund shower alone when he's at my place

shut up

this is why he's never going to kill your husband for you

i don't see anybody killing your husband

well it's hard to see
when you're blinded
by jealousy

oh guess what edmund came out of the shower
he says he loves me and we're getting married and he's going to
murder my husband
so

can't talk gotta go bye!!!

you're lying

nope he's killing my husband right now
oh my god there's so much blood
we're going to have to take another shower
after all this husband
murdering
byyyyye

don't you dare
goneril
goneril
you made that up right
i'm calling right now

■ ■ ■

let's just run away, Cordelia

all right

you and me
we'll run off to jail together
Lear and Cordelia, together again

oh

just the two of us
like birds in a cage
I'll be one bird and you'll be the other bird

huh

we can laugh at butterflies

and listen to court gossip from the guards
and just live there forever
and pray and sing and laugh
we'll be SPIES for GOD
just like two crazy birds trapped in a tower together

yeah
that would be
jail with my dad
so much better than moving to France
with my powerful new husband
yeah
wow

forever and ever
it'll be so great
let's do it

oh
okay
yes
sure
let me just
tell my husband that
I'm running off to jail with my dad forever

okay i'll wait

it might take a little while
things are pretty crazy around here right now

be right here
whenever you get back

John Donne

i just think it's a little weird
you don't mind when a flea bites both of us
but you won't have sex with me
i wouldn't even bite you

what

unless you wanted me to
obviously if you wanted me to i would bite you
but the biting's really not the point here

i didn't let the flea bite me
i didn't even know it was there

see
that's just how easy having sex with me is
wait
that's not
that's not exactly what i mean

i really don't see what the flea has to do with us

it means we're basically married
it has my blood and your blood in it
so
you've technically already had sex with me
and you might as well do it again

i don't
wait
but there could be a lot of other blood in there too

well we might have to have sex with all those people too

what

don't get mad at me
get mad at the flea for making me have sex with so many people

look i'll just kill the flea
okay?
the flea is gone

oh my god you'll kill our blood baby
but you won't even have sex with me

Hamlet

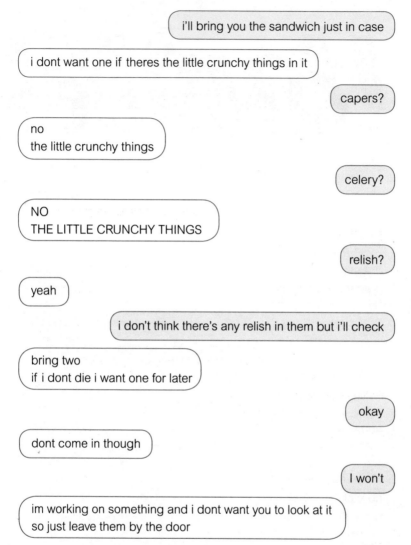

i'll bring you the sandwich just in case

i dont want one if theres the little crunchy things in it

capers?

no
the little crunchy things

celery?

NO
THE LITTLE CRUNCHY THINGS

relish?

yeah

i don't think there's any relish in them but i'll check

bring two
if i dont die i want one for later

okay

dont come in though

I won't

im working on something and i dont want you to look at it
so just leave them by the door

Don Quixote

Dulcinea
DULCINEA
BESTIR YOURSELF
dragons -
dragons everywhere -

where are there dragons?
where are you?

I am beset by dragons, my love!
there has been perfidy
in this strange land of iron islands
and wraiths that drape themselves in steam

are you in the kitchen?

no kitchen could produce a bellow so terrifying
nor a stench so foul
as that of these steel dragons

i think you are in the kitchen

they perch upon nests of flame!!

yes
you are absolutely in the kitchen
that is the tea kettle

I WILL SLAY THEM ALL

please do not stab my tea kettle

ah, dear one
your concern for my safety does you credit
but a man must be brave
where is my steed
where is Rocinante
I REQUIRE SWIFTNESS

Hamlet

Part II

Did you just take a tray up to him

up to who?

Don't do that

don't do what

Pretend you don't know who I'm talking about

well he needs to eat
I don't know what to tell you
he's a growing boy and he needs to eat

How old is he?

I don't understand what that's supposed to mean

I mean
how old does he have to get before he stops growing

People are always growing

He's 37

He's still in school!

He can eat dinner with us like a normal human being or he can wait until breakfast like everyone else

I can't believe you

Maybe if you didn't let him sleep in until noon he'd be hungry at dinner

Maybe if you talked to him he wouldn't want to stay in his room all the time

René Descartes

are you up
i can't sleep
what if there's an evil demon as clever and deceitful as he is powerful
who has directed his entire effort to misleading me

> i don't know
> i guess that would be awful
> go back to sleep

what if that's just what the evil demon wants me to do

> i don't know

oh my god
what if i'm asleep already
what if i'm dreaming right now
and all of my perceptions are false

> i don't know
> then I guess it doesn't matter
> so you might as well just go back to sleep

how can you think of sleep at a time like this

> well i usually am asleep at three in the morning
> it's a habit of mine

maybe you just think it's a habit of yours
maybe the evil demon is deceiving you too

maybe

what is a dream but a series of lies designed to keep us
immobilized in a dark room for hours at a time

that's a good point
i'm going to go back to sleep and i'll think about that while i'm
dreaming

that sounds like something an evil demon would say

guess I'll just have to take that chance

are you really going back to sleep
are you sleeping
don't go to sleep
i want to talk about math

William Wordsworth

hi

hey

how are you

pretty good thanks!

good
good
thats good
im glad someones doing good today
thats good
for you

how are you doing, William?

oh dont worry about me

I'm not worried

no need to worry about how im doing

I'm just asking
how you're doing

ahhhhhhhhh
i just feel like
a cloud
you know?
like a cloud looking at flowers

oh
I'm sorry?

just a lonely old cloud
made of vapor and sadness
and whatever else clouds are made of
looking at flowers
wandering
alone

William
do you want me to come over?

no
i dont care
i dont want to bother you

it's no trouble

how can you even visit a cloud
too busy wandering
lonely
over hills and things

do you want me to come over?

that would be nice
yes
please

Hamlet

Part III

they had the little crunchy things in them

oh honey I'm sorry
I thought I picked all of them out

well
you didnt

do you want something else?

no

are you sure?

i ate them anyway
they were okay i guess
i guess i dont mind the little crunchy things that much
:)

that girl keeps calling for you by the way

tell her im not here

are you sure?

yes im busy

im working on my project

let me just come in for five minutes so I can vacuum for you
I promise I won't get in the way of your project

DON'T COME IN MY ROOM

okay
okay I won't
I'm sorry honey
Hamlet?
honey?

Samuel Taylor Coleridge

what if the moon was haunted
by women who had sex with demons

what

what if kubla khan made a whole dome
just for pleasure
and put an ocean underneath the ground
with no sun in it

wow
i don't know

and rivers flung boulders up out of the earth at people
haha
flung 'em right up at people's stupid faces

i guess that would really be something

you're damn right it'd be something
caves of ice
and ancestral war voices prophesying about damsels
and sacred rivers screaming beware
and your hair would float
and
ugh hang on
two seconds
there's a guy here

ok

be right back

■ ■ ■

you still there?

uuuuugh
that guy

who was it?

some asshole from Porlock

what did he want

to talk to me for like
a million hours
about nothing
apparently
anyhow
what was i saying
fuck
what was i saying

something about a river

no
that wasn't it
fuuuuuck
hey do you have any opium

Hamlet

Part IV

> your friends are here to see you
> do you want me to send them up?

they're not my real friends
if they were really my friends theyd leave me alone

> your girlfriend's here with them
> should she leave you alone too?

first of all
she's not my girlfriend
second of all
denmark is a PRISON

> maybe if you left your room
> it wouldn't seem so much like one
> maybe if you went outside
> or just came down to dinner maybe

stop telling me what to do
you're a fascist
everything is such bullshit
men
women
animals
the sky
you
such bullshit

Part II

Jane Eyre

> JANE
> MY LITTLE SUNBEAM
> WHERE ARE YOU
> I NEED YOU BY MY SIDE

> I'm taking a walk
> be back for dinner

> AH YES MY CAGED SPRITE
> COMMUNE WITH NATURE AND UPON YOUR RETURN
> RELATE TO ME THE VAGRANT GLORIES OF THE
> RUINED WOODS

> do you really want me to describe my walk to you

> MORE THAN ANYTHING YOU POCKET WITCH

> it is fairly cloudy out
> looks like rain soon

> AHHH TO THINK THAT MY LITTLE STARLING JANE
> SHOULD RETURN
> TO PERCH ON MY BROKEN MALFORMED SHOULDER
> SINGING A SONG OF THE GREY AND WRACKING SKIES
> MAKES MY HEART SWELL TO BURST

> all right

JANE
JANE I BOUGHT YOU A DRESS MADE OF TEN
THOUSAND PEARLS AS A BRIDAL PRESENT

where on earth would I wear that

YOU COULD WEAR IT ON THE MOON

that seems impractical
how would i even breathe on the moon?

I WOULD BREATHE FOR YOU MY JANE
JANE WHERE HAVE YOU GONE
I AM BEREFT AND WITHOUT MY JANE
I SHALL SINK INTO ROGUERY

i am with my cousins

WHICH COUSIN
IS IT THE SEXY ONE

Please don't try to talk to me again

IT IS YOUR SEXY COUSIN
"ST. JOHN"
WHAT KIND OF A NAME IS ST. JOHN

I'm not going to answer that

I KNEW IT
DID YOU LEAVE BECAUSE OF MY ATTIC WIFE
IS THAT WHAT THIS IS ABOUT

yes
Absolutely

BECAUSE MY HOUSE IN FRANCE DOESN'T EVEN HAVE AN
ATTIC
IF THAT'S WHAT YOU WERE WORRIED ABOUT
IT HAS A CELLAR THOUGH SO YOU KNOW
DON'T CROSS ME
HAHA I'M ONLY JOKING

I hope you're packed for India already

I'm not going to India with you, St. John

That's not what these TWO TICKETS TO INDIA say

You know I don't want to marry you
Why don't you marry Rosamond instead?
Take her with you

Marry her?
MARRY HER?
Don't be ridiculous
I'm attracted to her
That's disgusting
You are disgusting, Jane

So you're really not coming then

I'm really not

I would be an amazing husband
you know that?

I know

I taught you Hindi and everything
That's basically the same as getting engaged
for missionaries

And I really appreciate that
It will be terribly useful in my career as an English governess

See?
That
There.
that is exactly the kind of tone I mean
One round of cholera in the tropics would sear
that sarcasm right out of you

guess I really missed out

Guess so

Sherlock Holmes

this is quite a puzzle, Watson

damned right, Holmes
hell of a puzzle
what I want to know is how did the vicar know the archbishop's
Pekingese had developed an immunity to snake bites?

there's only one thing we're missing
only one thing we need that will help us solve this case

we need to question Lady Emily again

no, Watson

oh
it's not
. . .

COCAINE, WATSON

ah

we're going to need loads of cocaine
SCADS of it

Sherlock, the others are already on their way
We've got to meet them at the museum

I yes
yes yes yes definitely for yes will be there
just give me five minutes for an errand
to do
five minutes

Sherlock please don't
Sherlock?
Christ
at least tell me where you are
so I can come get you

■ ■ ■

I'm sorry Lestrade
I don't think he's coming
I've tried calling him but he's not picking up
it's snowing
and I don't think he took a coat with him

■ ■ ■

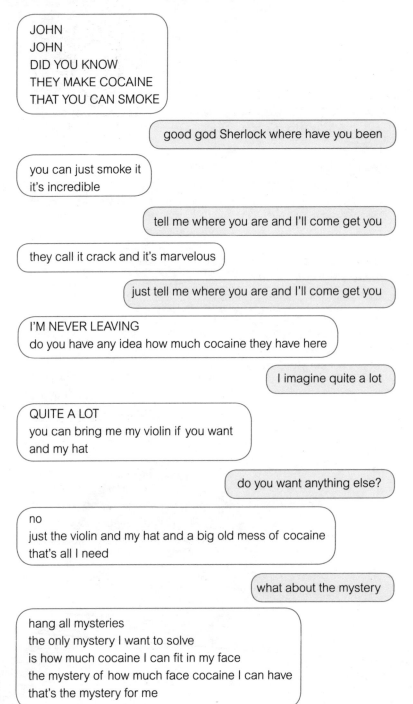

JOHN
JOHN
DID YOU KNOW
THEY MAKE COCAINE
THAT YOU CAN SMOKE

good god Sherlock where have you been

you can just smoke it
it's incredible

tell me where you are and I'll come get you

they call it crack and it's marvelous

just tell me where you are and I'll come get you

I'M NEVER LEAVING
do you have any idea how much cocaine they have here

I imagine quite a lot

QUITE A LOT
you can bring me my violin if you want
and my hat

do you want anything else?

no
just the violin and my hat and a big old mess of cocaine
that's all I need

what about the mystery

hang all mysteries
the only mystery I want to solve
is how much cocaine I can fit in my face
the mystery of how much face cocaine I can have
that's the mystery for me

Emily Dickinson

I saw –
Today –
a Cricket Man,

okay

he did not stop to Chat —

is that it
did anything else happen

No –

let's go out tonight okay
we don't have to do anything big but I think we should go out
just for dinner or something
I think that would be a good idea

Go out, Again? -
I went Out to Mount Holyoke

for college
you went there for college thirteen years ago

And now I must rest.

■ ■ ■

have you seen –
my Shawl

which shawl

the White shawl

I thought you were wearing your white shawl

a person can have more than one white Shawl
a person cannot be content with but one white Shawl

i think i saw it downstairs

Alas

just on the couch

You know I do not go downed Stairs
I will knit a new one

that's ridiculous

when I die
I wish to be buried in that Shawl
I wish to be buried — in ten Thousand Shawls –

you're not dying
you're just afraid of the stairs

No Coward Soul Is Mine
I fear no Step'd Floor

do you want me to just bring it to you

if you are already going to be coming Upstairs
will you also grab my slippers by the Door
and also –

yes?

some — Tea

okay

also there are four more Shawls on the stairs
bring those too

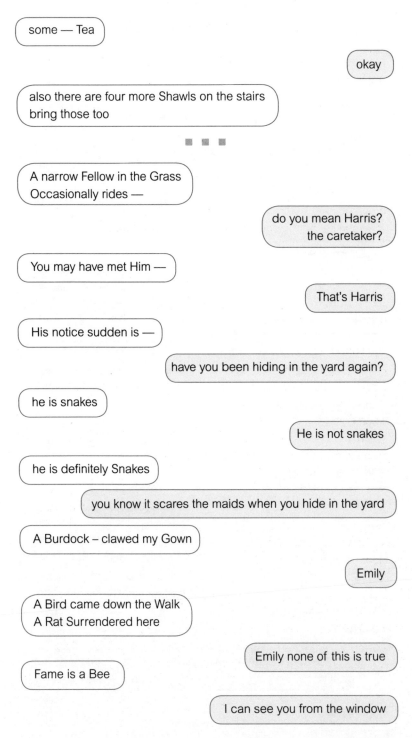

A narrow Fellow in the Grass
Occasionally rides —

do you mean Harris?
the caretaker?

You may have met Him —

That's Harris

His notice sudden is —

have you been hiding in the yard again?

he is snakes

He is not snakes

he is definitely Snakes

you know it scares the maids when you hide in the yard

A Burdock – clawed my Gown

Emily

A Bird came down the Walk
A Rat Surrendered here

Emily none of this is true

Fame is a Bee

I can see you from the window

nothing's clawing at you or surrendering

a soft Sea is washing around the house
I haven't told the Garden yet

Emily why don't you come inside

A Toad can die of Light, you know

I know
why don't you come inside
I'll get your white shawl

which white Shawl

whichever one you want

I want the one in the library

okay
will you come inside then?

Toads can die of light you know

I believe you

Kills them right up

■ ■ ■

Emily
Emily, dearest
will you please let me in?
I just want to air out your room

Air has no Residence
no Neighbor

Emily, it's been an awfully long time since you came out
can I please come in?

not — Now –

When can I come in?

After a hundred years

Emily
will you give me a real amount of time, please?

After all Birds have been investigated and laid aside

do you have birds in there?

After the Sun comes out

Emily
answer the question

At Half past Three

how many birds are in there

A single Bird

this is why people don't visit us
the bird thing

Back from the cordial Grave I dragged him

is the bird still alive, Emily?

do you know what the Best witchcraft is?

Emily

Geometry

just tell me if the bird is still alive

COCOONS ABOVE
COCOONS BELOW

I'm coming in

COCOONS

Oliver Twist

please madam
it being Christmas and all
might I
if you would not object
might I be allowed to eat the cheese the rats have
left behind in the traps?

the rat-cheese?
you impertinent boy
that's the most important cheese of all
and later tonight
for asking the matron a question on a Sunday
I shall have you soundly killed

I understand

after you are killed I shall expect you to scrub the stairs

yes ma'am

then you shall clean out the grease-pans and report back
to Chumsley Fezzlethroat
and he shall kill you again before bed

does this mean i shan't have to sweep out the chimneys
with my own hair tonight ma'am

how dare you ask such a question
you dreadful, grimy boy
of course your head will be used to sweep out the chimneys
now go stand out in the rain until you have melted

yes ma'am

and no supper until you are thirty-five

yes ma'am

and after that the sixth-form boys will seize you about the ankles
and dip you into the electric loom at the mill
until you are torn to shreds

yes ma'am

then the shreds will be sent to work for a family of twelve
in Coventry
the family lives in an old boot
and you shall have to keep the boot spotlessly clean
and if I hear that any of your shreds have displeased
the household I shall ride a sledge of furious dogs
into your bedroom and read the book of Lamentations
aloud until you have been eaten alive
by the furious dogs

yes ma'am

Merry Christmas to you, then
run along, you little scamp

Merry Christmas, matron

I spoil you, you know
I shouldn't, but I can't help it
my heart's too easily touched

yes ma'am
thank you ma'am

Lord Byron

this guy
this publisher guy
is asking me about my favorite canto in Child Harolde
that's like asking someone to pick who's hotter
his half-sister or his cousins
it's literally impossible

■ ■ ■

hey
do you think we could just stay in tonight maybe
i'm so wiped out from last night
we could just stay in
get in our jammies and not see anyone
maybe build a fire

oh wow
really?

hahaha i'm kidding
there's already a sex pigeon in your room
i'm coming over in five minutes

oh

by the way
do you have that cream from before
the anti chafing cream
we're going to need a lot of it
to prevent chafing

oh okay

choirboys chafe easy imho

■ ■ ■

uuuuuuughhh
nothing's any good

what's the matter

EVERYTHING
do you realize i'm never going to be able to have sex with the rain

i didn't know you wanted to have sex with the rain

of course i want to have sex with the rain
how can you even say that
i feel like you don't even know me

maybe
you should focus
on all the things that you can have sex with

Yeah maybe
i just want to live you know

right

i want to have a threesome with the moon and jealousy

right

Yeah and i want to do it with the rain but i can't
uuuuuuuughhhh
i should just go die in Greece

what?

nothing

I wrote a poem today
do you want to hear it

okay

Near this Spot
are deposited the Remains of one
who possessed Beauty without Vanity,
Strength without Insolence,
Courage without Ferosity,
and all the virtues of Man without his Vices.
This praise, which would be unmeaning Flattery
if inscribed over human Ashes,
is but a just tribute to the Memory of
BOATSWAIN, a DOG,
who was born in Newfoundland May 1803
and died at Newstead Nov. 18, 1808.
hey totally unrelated
do you remember how many children i have?
i'm trying to do a tax thing right now
and i have nooooo idea haha
like
it's for sure SOME

no sorry

fuck
i gotta write some letters
uuuuuuuuuuuuuuuuuuuuuuuuuughhhhh

John Keats

oh my god
oh my god
do you know what I LOVE
like what I am just crazy about

is it this urn

THIS
URN

I figured
you seemed really excited

THIS GRECIAN URN

it's really pretty

FUCK OFF WITH THAT REALLY PRETTY BULLSHIT
IT'S THE BRIDE OF QUIETNESS
IT'S THE CHILD OF TIME AND OF SILENCE AND IT'S SO GOOD
IT'S LIKE IMAGINARY MUSIC
I FUCKING LOVE THIS URN SO MUCH
IT'S GOT A PRIEST ON IT
HE'S ALL MYSTERIOUS
FUCKIN MYSTERIOUS PRIEST
THERE'S A COW ON IT
WEARING FLOWERS
AND MAIDENS
IT'S GOT TRUTH ON IT
THIS URN TELLS THE GODDAMN TRUTH
IT'S SO BEAUTIFUL

right, right

FUCK YOU
ARE YOU EVEN LOOKING AT IT

I am
I am looking at it

ARE YOU REALLY LOOKING AT IT

I am
I swear

like really look at it though

okay
okay I will

good
Sorry

it's okay

I didn't mean to get so carried away

I know

I just love this urn
so much

it really is a great urn

it really is
i just love it so much

I know
it's okay

Emma

darling Emma
have you seen our friend Mr. Martin?
he was to take me to tea this afternoon but he isn't here

oh Harriet!
do you really still like him??

oh
I did
Yes

i told him you were not virtuous
and i think that got rid of him
i didn't think you still liked him
you wouldn't have liked him for much longer anyhow
lol what would your name even have been if
you married him
"Mrs. Farmer"??
that's not even a name, Harriet
"hi I'm Mrs. Farmer I'm married to a farm"
bugs live on farms, Harriet
also
for another thing
he is dreadful at whist
oooh
do you want to come over and play whist??

wait
i think it was Mr. Martin
i definitely told SOMEONE you were not virtuous
lollll
idk who exactly but
it was for sure definitely someone

■ ■ ■

Father
I want to make a new house rule
no more servants getting married
remember when Miss Taylor got married?
it was awful
we didn't have enough people in the house to play whist for weeks
anyhow
I guess what I'm trying to say is
I told Hannah she has to turn down Mr. Smith
I was firm but fair
she's the only one in the servant's hall to ever lead a grand slam
and she wanted to throw that away
just because she is with child
anyhow
want to come downstairs and play whist???

■ ■ ■

One new voicemail from Jane Fairfax
Press 7 to save your message
Press 8 to delete your message
88888888888888888

Command not recognized

8

Your message has been deleted

■ ■ ■

do you know what I can't stand

what

Pride and Prejudice

And you must see to it that your sister invites Mr. Bingley, Lizzie

He isn't here, Mother

Isn't here?
he must be here
the ball is in seven days
and if he is not here then how will we convince our
Mr. Darcy to attend?

Mr. Darcy is not here either

no?
but I thought he was in London
for business
and would return in time for the ball

No
he is not in London
he is on a ship
he is going to war

but this is terrible news

There is an actual war on right now
against Napoleon

how could this have happened??

He was commissioned months ago

And Mr. Bingley?

He is also there
He is also at the war that is happening now

oh my god
we are going to have to put off this ball

Probably yes

■ ■ ■

do you know who I miss?

Who?

Mr. Collins
remember Mr. Collins?
remember him?
remember when he visited?

I do
I do remember

what I liked about him the most
was how much he wanted to marry you
remember that?

Yes

remember when there was someone who wanted to marry you

Just

good God

if there is a man you are thinking of
under the age of 35
who is in the militia or an officer of any kind
he is probably at the war

is that where your friend Mary went too
the one who went missing

I don't think so

well you should check
apparently everyone is going there
apparently no one is going to balls anymore because they just
can't get enough of Napoleon

■ ■ ■

did you mean MARY?

did I mean what?

when you were talking about Mary earlier
were you talking about MARY Mary?

which Mary did you think I was talking about?

the tall one
the one who lives upstairs
with the glasses
the upstairs girl
who frowns at the piano

■ ■ ■

oh Jane i'm so happy for you

Thank you

and Lizzie too of course

Yes, that's wonderful

and now Lydia too
thank God you all found such wonderful men to marry

Thank you

we would all honestly be homeless right now if you hadn't

I suppose that's true

we would have nowhere to go
everyone we know would just
allow that to happen to us
I hope you don't think I was so hard on all of you about it
without cause

No of course not

It's just that if you didn't marry I would spend the rest of my life
worrying about my homeless daughters
I'm just glad we're all so happy now
and even if you aren't very happy
literally your only other options would have been prostitution or
begging
so

Let's not talk about it

Please have sons

all right, Mother

have sons and be happy

I know

I'm still going to lose the house
the minute your father dies
he'll just be dead and I'll have no husband
and no house and nothing

I know

I'm going to have to live with one of you
you're going to have let me move in with you
until I die

I know

Christ, it's awful

It really is

Moby-Dick

> HROOOOOOOARRRRRRRROOOOOOOOOGH

> good God in heaven

> what is this?

> HROOOOOOOOOOOOOOOOOOARRRRRRGGGGGHHHOO
> OOOORROOOOOHHH

> it is the whale
> it is the whale!
> Bellow all you like
> this boat never sheers off from anything that wears the
> shape of a whale

> LOLLLLLL no
> it's just me

margarine!
who would have guessed

I do not know, Captain

so for starters
you actually have to hydrogenate it
which I know sounds crazy but that's how you get rid of
that fishy smell

I see

you know that fish smell I mean
like what everything smells like right now

■ ■ ■

do you realize we could be back on Martha's Vineyard in like six
hours?
maybe eight
in less than a day we could be having dinner on Martha's Vineyard

after we have slain the whale, of course?

ugh
yes sure fine
whatever
we could be there in eight hours, is all I'm saying

only after you have burst the hot heart of the mighty whale
with spears and with knives and harpoons
and we bear its carcass triumphantly back to shore

uuugh
it's like always harpoons with you Ishmael

hey what are you doing
like right now

> i am shrouded in blackness
> in ten times black
> i am tending to the oil vats and stripping the fat

awesome
awesome
that sounds awesome

> Do you need something from me, Captain?

not really
I guess not
are you with Queequeg right now

> he is in his bunk
> recovering from his brush with death

cool cool
will you tell him I say hi?

> certainly

great
it's not a big deal or anything
you can make it sound casual
ask him what he's doing for dinner
if he wants to have dinner in the captain's quarters
with me obviously
haha
like obviously I wouldn't ask him to just have dinner
by himself in a weird new part of the ship all alone

Is there any other message I should give him?

hmm?

About the hunt tomorrow?

hunt tomorrow

For the whale
For the white whale
for the white whale, or the devil

yesss oh yes definitely
yes for sure that is still on
whales whales whales
I am super prepared for whales
Tomorrow

I will tell him
Would you like me to ask him if he will attend the hunt, then?

oh my God
why so many Queequeg questions

Captain?

you're just
asking a lot of questions about him is all
it's kind of like you're obsessed with him or something

■ ■ ■

do you ever worry
that the whale is like
a metaphor

a metaphor?

yeah

sometimes

me too
me too
do you wanna nail stuff to the mast?

yeah

ok

be there in five

■ ■ ■

Sir, the crew begs that you leave off your mad pursuit
We are sick from it, we are sick to the point of perishing
We must return to port

oh
yes
terribly mad
I'm just mad for
revenge and so on
all types of revenge for my legs, and whatnot

Sir?

leg
just the leg
he only took the one leg right

Captain, I do not know what the whale took from you

oh I'm just
furious about it
the legs, I mean
and the whale

Please

Did you know that the digestive organs of the whale are so inscrutably constructed that it is quite impossible for him to completely digest even a man's arm?

I didn't

well it's true
think about that
think about that the next time you're thinking about whales

Great Expectations

Sarah, darling!
Got your note

oh lovely

couldn't possibly make it over for the christening
as I'm simply swamped at the moment
(you may recall I was left at the altar
and have spent the intervening years reeling from the betrayal)

yes I remember

Wish terribly I could make it
but you know how it is
being jilted

Well
we'll set out a piece of cake for you just in case

Please don't worry about me
I'm surrounded by the ruins of an aching, hopeless love that's
slowly congealing into poison
so I'm keeping busy
much love to the baby

thank you

if it's a boy I hope you drown it

■ ■ ■

Pip
Pip what are you doing right now

> I'm at work
> what's up

did you know that my name would have been Mrs. Compeyson
if I'd married my fiancé Mr. Compeyson

> really

but I never did marry him

> right

because as you recall
I was abandoned on my wedding day
by my fiancé
(Mr. Compeyson)
and have never never
never recovered
but I'm just thrilled to hear that you're doing so well
just Havisham will do for now
unless he comes back

> is there anything in particular you need from me right now?

all men are dogs Pip

> okay

write that down

> I will

really write it down though
are you writing it down?

Gone with the Wind

where r u

Scarlett I'm at work
I can't text right now

need u at mill

Scarlett I have the baby with me I really can't come to the mill

what baby

My baby.
Beau. My baby with Melanie.

guess what kind of corset im wearing

I don't see what this has to do with

im not ;)

■ ■ ■

Darling, I was going through some old things this morning
and found Charles' ornamental officer's sash
I thought you'd like to have it
So I gave it to Mammy for cleaning and she'll give it to you later

who is charles

Scarlett, how you joke!

was he that guy

I know it pains you to speak of him
that's why you act so high-spirited about it
and I think it's simply marvelous of you
But you don't have to be brave with me, Scarlett dear

that guy with like the chin thing

I miss him too

guess what i turned my mourning gown into

But I know he's looking after us — always

i made four backless shimmies out of it

■ ■ ■

mammy
mammy r u up

What is it, Scarlett

do we have any of that chocolate stuff left
with the swirls on it

I don't know, Scarlett

can you check

Honey, I'll get it for you just as soon as the doctor lets me
get out of bed
He says the typhoid is awfully bad this spring

what even is typhoid

It's nothing
I've got a little touch of it is all
but I'll be fine, don't you worry

haha omg ur gonna get so thin
my waist is like nineteen inches already im a whale
listen to me talking about that chocolate stuff
don't let me have any!!!

All right

ok no but seriously bring me like one jar
just one though

■ ■ ■

4 missed calls

■ ■ ■

ohhh my god she will not stop CALLING
its like
im not a baby catcher ok
sorry ur "in labor" again or whatever
im in labor too
in the fields picking cotton or whatever the hell is growing
out of those bushes
ive had like four babies already, it's not a big deal AT ALL

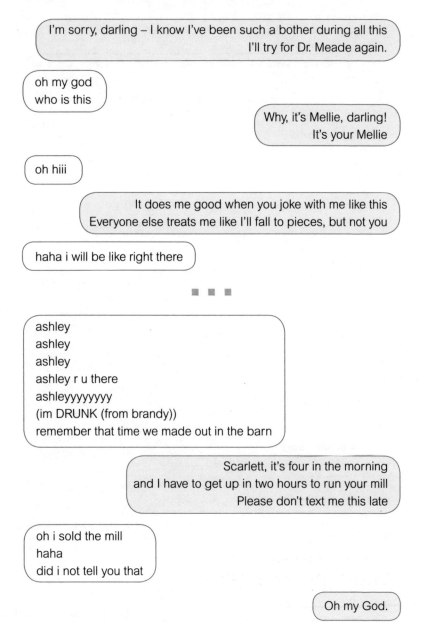

did you know that pantalets are out this year
that's why im not wearing any
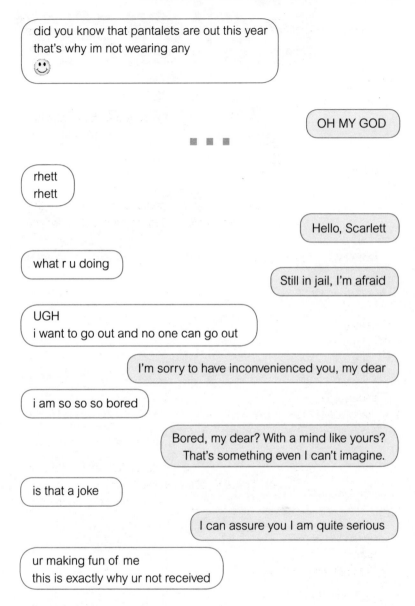

OH MY GOD

■ ■ ■

rhett
rhett

Hello, Scarlett

what r u doing

Still in jail, I'm afraid

UGH
i want to go out and no one can go out

I'm sorry to have inconvenienced you, my dear

i am so so so bored

Bored, my dear? With a mind like yours?
That's something even I can't imagine.

is that a joke

I can assure you I am quite serious

ur making fun of me
this is exactly why ur not received

Edgar Allan Poe

hey

where are you?

hi

where are you?
you're like two hours late
it's almost midnight

i can't get out of the house right now

is your car blocked?
do you need a ride?

no
it's like
there's this bird

there's a bird on your car?

no he's sitting on my statue
it's like
mm it just keeps looking at me
got those fiery bird eyes
you know?

what?

fired up eyebirds
you know
like how when a bird looks at you so much
that you can't leave the house

that's
no
that's never happened to me

well it's happening like crazy over here
so i have to keep looking at him
it might take a while
oh and plus i fell asleep reading
i was asleep for like an hour
i literally just woke up
and now i have this bird thing to deal with
so i don't think i'm going to make it tonight
sorry hun :)

▨ ▨ ▨

search Contacts for "Lenore"
Contact not found

▨ ▨ ▨

hey i'm going to be late to Kim's thing
can't really leave the house right now
save a seat for me though okay

is that bird still there?

no
lol what bird?
oh
yes
but that's not the point
the bird's fine, whatever
it's the bells

the bells?

yeah
the bells, bells, bells, bells,
bells, bells, bells-

what bells?

from the jingling and the tinkling of the bells

what bells are in your house?

oh man what kind of bells AREN'T here
mellow wedding bells
golden bells
loud alarum bells
brazen bells
terror bells

terror bells?

All kinds of bells
the anger of the bells
the horror of the bells
the iron bells
sobbing bells, bells, bells, bells, bells,
bells, bells, bells, bells

okay
okay I'll save you a seat

yeah definitely save me a seat though
i'm for sure going to make it
i just have to sit through the bells first

right

■ ■ ■

search Contacts for "Lost Lenore"
Contact not found

■ ■ ■

hey is Virginia going to be there

which Virginia?

the hot one

I don't know which one you mean

the one who's always sick
i think she has cholera
or tuberculosis or something

the tall one?

no

the redhead?

the one whose dad is brothers with my dad

your cousin Virginia?

lol idk how else you make cousins
except for having dads that are brothers
so yeah
oh

I don't know

save me a seat next to her okay
if she's coming

■ ■ ■

hiiiiiiiiiiiiiiii

Hi

ok don't be mad at me

why?

i feel like you're going to be mad at me
or like you're mad at me
or something
so don't be mad at me

you're not coming

i can't coooome to the thiiiiing tonight
i'm so sorry

you can't leave the house?

oh my god
i canNOT leave the house

I feel like that's turning into a thing with you

what do you mean

well
like last week
you couldn't leave the house
because you were too busy looking at a bird
is it the bird thing again?

hi
whoa
hi
whoa
i wasn't LOOKING at a bird
wow where is this even coming from
the BIRD
wouldn't stop LOOKING
at ME

okay

that's a really big difference
anyone can look at a bird
i could go look at a bird right now if i wanted
i could go look at the same bird
he's still fucking here
not that you asked

I literally just did ask

fuck you

why can't you leave the house

oh my god
where to even START
there's a heart in the floor
and it will not shut uppppp of beating
but that's not even the main thing
there's a cat with one eye that keeps calling me a murderer

well
did you murder anyone?

wow
you know what you sound like right now?

do I sound like the cat

you sound like the cat with one eye

I'm just asking because you said you had a heart in the floor

I said there WAS a heart in the floor
not that i HAD a heart in the floor
there are a lot of reasons a person could have a heart in their floor
not just murder reasons
thanks a lot though

Treasure Island

finddd
you want to know where the treasure is?
i don,t care
i dont care
i'll tell you

You will?

tell you about treasures
tell you about all the treasures i wanna tell you about

Thank you
Thank you so much
this could end the fighting between the men

no but Jim
Jim Jim Jim Jim
Listen

I'm listening
I'm ready

listen to me
the real treasure is friendship, Jim
you and me is the real treasure
if I could rename Treasure Island
Id call it my friend jim island
I would

■ ■ ■

jim
jim remINd me
how many legs do you have

John...

no no no no yes
how many legs
do you have under your body
like for walking

I'm sorry
I shouldn't have brought it up

is it two
because if it's two

yes

are either of them A STICK

it's two

then sounds to me like you're one LUCKY Jim

■ ■ ■

♦

SWEET CHRIST
THE BLACK SPOT

ahahahha

This is a joke to you?
You laugh?
This is my death warrant

♦

what devilry is this?
how came you by this symbol?

it's emojiiiis

■ ■ ■

hey jimbles

yes?

theres a LOT of things you can bury you know
not just treasure

what have you been burying?

nothinnnnnnng

what have you buried?

idk
what can't you bury jim
im just saying if you want to bury something besides treasure
you probably can
what are you doing right now
jim?
hey can u look something up for me
how long do birds live
specifically parrots

■ ■ ■

jim
jim
jim
jim
jim r u awake
jimmmmmmm
sleepy jimmy i gotta
i gotta tell you something
you can't maroon your problems jim
thats your problem
jim you can maroon some of the people some of the time
and you can maroon all of the people some of the time
wait thats not right
because if you maroon everyone
then its not really marooning
because everyone's all there together
look jim
Jim shut up
the point is
the point is you can't keep marooning your feelings
your problems
whichever
my problem is that one of my legs is a stick
plus i have all this treasure i stole
but your problem is
you got real problems lucky jim
you up?
i'm coming over i bet youre up

Gone with the Wind

Part II

Prissy
it's been hours since the men left
and there's still no sign of the O'Haras
how ever did you manage it

well I had to buy time, you know
so Sam and the others could change out of their
Confederate uniforms
and escape
so I told her
I'd help with the baby
when Melanie's time came

You didn't!

I did
but then wouldn't you know it?
it turns out
I don't know a thing about birthing babies

you're terrible

I'm afraid I wasn't very helpful at all
and slowed things down considerably

Prissy, you're a marvel

Try growing cotton this year on salted farmland, Miss O'Hara

Prissy!

You know, I suppose Scarlett was right
The Yankees couldn't take Tara
and the carpetbaggers couldn't take Tara
But I could

Part III

"The Yellow Wallpaper"

Poppet
I couldn't help but notice
that the gate at the top of the stairs was ajar

Oh?

which suggests to me
that a certain someone
has been going downstairs
can you think of who that might be?

Oh dear
Oh John, I'm sorry
I called for you but you weren't at home
no one was home
and I was so thirsty

Darling
you know that going downstairs makes you hysterical

I know

It's called a rest cure, my love
Not a going downstairs cure

How right you are

you'd better stay in bed this time
or someone's going to lose her sitting up in bed privileges

I'm sorry

little goose

■ ■ ■

John
couldn't I go outside even for a little while
just for a walk in the garden
just for a moment

why must you ask for the moon
you know I wish I could give it to you
but I might as well feed you poison
a walk in the garden is the last thing you need
it might undo you entirely, garden walking

I just can't bear another minute staring at these same walls

anything can happen to a woman in a garden

This wallpaper
it's strange
I can't bear it

I'm afraid that as a doctor
I can't advise going out into the garden
it's full of night humors and cross-breezes
any one of which could do any number of things to your nervous
system to say nothing of your chalkstones
it would simply ruin your blood

all right

I'm afraid I just can't allow it

all right

but I could have Nurse bring you a bowl of arrowroot
that's almost as good
isn't it?
a bowl of arrowroot's almost as good as walking

all right

■ ■ ■

What do you think we should name the child?

Oh, John, I'm so glad you asked
I've missed talking to someone
and I do hope the baby's doing well
I've thought about it a great deal these last few months

oh sorry, darling
that wasn't for you
meant to send that to Williams
think we've found a fine name for him anyhow

It's a boy?
I had
We had a son?
What's his name, darling?
John?
What's his name?

I'll tell you what, my darling
You've been awfully good this week
and I think you deserve a treat

What's that?

you can have all the air that you want
I know
I spoil you

you'll open one of the windows, then?
I would so love to see the sky again

Good God, no
not FRESH air
Good lord
do you want to catch winter fever?

But it's summer, John
surely it couldn't be as bad as all that in the summer

Summer is the worst time of all to catch winter fever
the body simply doesn't expect it
Next thing you know
your dropsy is so bilious it makes ship fever look like barrel fever
And then where would you be

I'm not sure
where would I be?

Nowhere good
I can tell you that much
nowhere good, medically speaking
no I'll have the air brought in downstairs and let it waft up
Go back to sleep

I've been asleep all morning
and all night before that
I couldn't possibly sleep any more
I'll go mad if I try to lie still another hour

ah that's how you know you need rest
only a truly sleepy woman would say that

■ ■ ■

John have you noticed a yellow smell in the house
I've noticed a yellow smell

A yellow smell?
Not particularly
Could be some sort of miasma
I'll have the garden torn up just in case
and extra bars set on the windows

■ ■ ■

darling
you know the broken-necked reverse-eyed witch nightmares in the
wallpaper?

the what?

you know the ones I mean, John dear
they writhe in those slinking hate patterns?

good God

Well they've started to chant in unison

what has become of you alone up there

Oh, don't worry, pet
I know how to quiet them
I know how to make them stop their needle dance
They promised me
once I've done what they want
they'll be at peace again
So there's nothing to worry about!
I'll be right down, darling
coming downstairs at last

Wuthering Heights

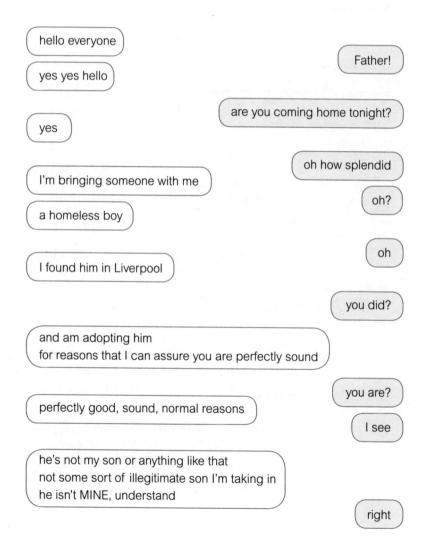

I'm just adopting him
it's not important how I found him or who his mother is
or what letters of mine she does or doesn't have
let's have no questions about the boy from now on
my favorite, special, beloved son,
who I adopted and definitely am not the real father of
be home in five!!!
(with the boy)
(his name is Heathcliff!!!)
(you're going to LOVE him)

■ ■ ■

god i love you cathy

> i love you too
> i love you so much
> god
> it hurts how much i love you

i love you so much
let's break each other's hearts

> oh my god let's
> i love you so much i'm going to marry edgar

i love you so much i'm going to run away

> i love you so much i'm going to make myself sick

good
good that's so much love

> i love you so much i'm going to get sick again
> just out of spite
> i'll forget how to breathe

i'll be your slave

god yes

and i'll bankroll your brother's alcoholism

i always hoped you would

uuuuuuugh

do you know who i hate?

everyone?

EVERYONE

☺ ☺ ☺

i love you SO MUCH
i'm going to write your name all over my books and then
i'm going to have someone else's baby and then DIE

yes
cathy yes that's perfect
i'm going to kidnap your daughter someday
and i won't let your nephew learn how to read
because of how much i love you
and scream at your grave
and i'll rent your room out
to some guy from London

oh my god thank you
thank you so much
i'm going to love you so much
i become a ghost

i'm so glad to hear that
i was hoping you'd say that

but i'm never going to haunt you

just that guy who's visiting from london

that sounds perfect
i'm so excited to hear him tell me about what your ghost looks like

oh my god
what are you going to scream at my grave

oh man
what aren't i going to scream at your grave
i'll scream everything
i'll scream at your soul

good good

i'll scream about what a bitch you were

i am so excited
i am going to just
ruin heaven with my screaming back at you

that is so sweet of you to do that

i'll just murder everyone's heart

i hope your ghost drives me crazy 😊

i love you like how rocks love forests

i totally know what you mean

i love you like i love the inside of my own brain

oh my god that's so much love

i knooooow
do you want to make out right now

god no
i want to wait until you're dead
and then rip up the earth over your grave
and crawl inside
IN MEMORY OF
CATHERINE

Little Women

MEG
MEG
MEG WHAT'S ALL THIS
WHAT'S ALL THIS I'M HEARING ABOUT YOUR GETTING
MARRIED
tell me it's a wretched lie

> Jo I don't know how many more times we have to have this conversation

I'll have it a THOUSAND TIMES if I must

> but yes
> I am still marrying John tomorrow

OH GREAT TRIPLE-HORNED GOD

> just like I was planning to yesterday

this is unbearable

> and also last month

answer me this, then
who exactly do you think is going to play Mercy
when we put on my version of The Pilgrim's Progress this
summer?
I wrote that part for YOU

wrote it beautifully in fact

I don't know, darling

she gets a cracking scene with the villain
Rodrigo where he tries to poison her
and she screams and faints and everything

I don't remember anyone named Rodrigo in The Pilgrim's Progress

THAT'S NEITHER HERE NOR THERE MEG

I'm very sorry

this production will be ruined

why don't you ask Amy?

i'm not even going to dignify that with a response

■ ■ ■

You still have three hours to change your mind
we could run away and be pirates
or just wear bloomers

but I love him, Jo

uuuuugh
I can't even understand you when you get hysterical like this

I love him and I want to marry him — that's all

you're just ranting now
it's pure gibberish

we'll be living just down the road, honestly
it'll be like i never left at all

does he have a horse?
is that what this is about?
does he have a sword gun or a railroad
or a
a nice hat or something?

no, that's not what this is about

I hope you realize you're breaking up the family

I really wish you wouldn't see things that way

a broken home
that's what I come from now
a broken home

that's not what they call it when your sister gets married

then why does it feel broken, Meg
why does it feel broken
this is the worst thing
that has ever happened
to anyone
since Father died

Father didn't die, Jo!

oh
didn't he?
for some reason I thought he'd died

no
he'll be home in a few weeks

Ah
do you suppose he's going to want his old greatcoat
and riding boots

and shaving things
and top hat
when he gets back?

I expect that he will

HANG EVERYTHING

■ ■ ■

LAURIE
I despise everything
did you know Meg wouldn't even let me have any fireworks at her
wedding

I didn't know that

not a single solitary firework
nor a footrace either
she wouldn't even let me challenge the groomsmen to a feat of
strength

well I'm afraid that's fairly customary
not to have the maid of honor wrestling the wedding party, I mean

THEN I'M NEVER GETTING MARRIED

all right

imagine having to get married without even one little roman
candle
i won't do it you know
i won't live in that kind of a world

all right, Jo

i'll kill myself and all of you
but i won't live in that world

■ ■ ■

amy?

yes?

amy im dying tonight

oh beth
No

yes im definitely dying
oh its terrible how much im dying just now

but
what exactly
what are you dying of

this sewing needle
it's so very heavy

well
put it down

the window
it's so
so bright

the window is killing you?

it's so terribly full of glass

I see

theres just glass all over it
i don't know how you stand it

oh
I manage

i dont think ill make it through the night

well I'll be here if you need me

and to think i once stepped outside the house
to stand in the sun

yes, I remember that day

what a strong and foolhardy girl i was then

dear Laurie
dearest Laurie
surely at this point you know
i can't possibly marry you
i'm so sorry
please try to forgive me

Jo
of course I'll respect your wishes
but why?
there's no one who knows you better

i know that

we have such fun together

we do!

and you're dear to me
and jolly

and clever
cleverer than me anyhow
and I
I do love you
most awfully, Jo

Laurie, I can't
please don't ask me again

I can't help but ask

and I can't give you any answer but no

all right
all right

■ ■ ■

Oh Meg, darling
it's all over
Beth is with Father now

Jo, Father still isn't dead

really?

I saw him not four hours ago

could have sworn he died at sea
or somewhere

■ ■ ■

Jo, I'm sorry about what I said the other day
I know how you feel about marriage
and — and everything

Oh, Laurie

that's all right

you'll never marry anyone
your writing is too important
that comes first

oh

I do admire you for that, really I do
you're going to do tremendous things

that's awfully kind of you to say

and I count myself lucky to know you
I do, Jo
we'll be old bachelors together
you and I

well
ah
the thing is, chum

running a cattle ranch
somewhere out West

turns out I am going to be married after all
I've met someone, I mean
please understand I never intended to
he's the most wonderful man
very old
much older than me

oh

he's German
very German

so German it's hard to understand him at first when he speaks

> and you're going to marry
> him
> with yourself
> you're going to be marrying him yourself I mean

his mustache is enormous
bushy and gray and covered in crumbs
all of him is covered in crumbs
he's filthy haha

> well that's just

oh and he just hates my writing
criticizes my work unceasingly

> I see

i really cannot overemphasize
how much he disapproves of my voice as a writer
wants me to change everything about it

> well
> how can I compete with that

exactly
please don't blame yourself

Hamlet

Part V

darling I don't mean to criticize but
you really hurt your father's feelings last night

hes not my real dad
why do you even like him

Henry David Thoreau

im going to the woods ok

okay

im going to live deliberately
with essential facts
im going to suck all the marrow out of the trees

okay

so dont follow me

how long are you going?

i dont know
however long it takes to live deliberately
so maybe a few months
or maybe forever gonna live in a cabin

well
i'm happy for you

can i use your cabin

you want to live in my cabin?

well i dont have a cabin
i need to be self sufficient
so i need to use your cabin

■ ■ ■

hey do you mind if i have some friends over to the cabin

how's it going out there
are you living deliberately

yeah pretty deliberately i guess
but its pretty boring out here without friends over

i guess so
as long as you keep things tidy
there's not room for many other people

no for sure for sure for sure
just the alcotts
and the hawthornes
and ellery is already here

he is?

yeah he sleeps on the floor by me
plus people are always stopping by to see me
and my self sufficient cabin

you mean my self sufficient cabin

the self sufficient cabin
anyhow
i invited a lot of them to spend the night too
the more the merrier thats my motto
just me and the lonely whispering of the wind among the reeds
and also the alcotts and the hawthornes
and my best friend ellery
and anyone else who happens to come by

that's
a lot of people

twenty five or thirty souls, with their bodies,
at once under my roof
give or take

hey do you want to come over
i just stole some pies

what

this lady just left out pies on her porch
so i took em
self sufficiently

i don't think that's very self sufficient

well i don't think you're very
shut up just come over
just come over to the damn woods

you know what i think are brave

what

minks
and muskrats
awfully brave
not like the great mass of mankind

what's so brave about them

you wouldn't understand
hey would you bring some more molasses if you're coming back
tomorrow
im all out

how much molasses do you need

i dont know
obviously
clearly if id known from the beginning i wouldn't need more now
so i guess "more" is the answer

why don't you just come over
and you can get all the molasses you need
and you can stay in town for a few nights
i think maybe that would be a good idea

no way man
no way
your life is a hollow shell
no offense but id rather die than stay at your house
just bring the molasses when you come over tomorrow
and also some more shoes because i lost the last pair
and some books
and pens i need pens
but thats it
and a thing of beans
thats for sure it

■ ■ ■

do you know whos my family ralph

who

these squirrels
these squirrels and this chipmunk and that crow over there

the crow on the chimney?

NO
not that one
god i hate that one
hes not my family
hes a fucking asshole

Daisy Miller

hey daisy
you look so good in that green dress today!!
so glad you're wearing it

thank you!

quick question
were you going to wear it like
to dinner?

i was
Yes

or is it like
a "joke"
i thought maybe it was a joke

no

what makes you ask?

oh my god
no reason at allll
totally just asking
it looks so good on you
and i think you're super brave for wearing it

brave?
why brave?

ahahahhahaha you are such a KIDDER
you and that green dress
not that i'd really call it a dress
see you at dinner!!!
see you and also i guess see that dress at dinner!!

The Island of Dr. Moreau

what do you think would happen
if you mixed a hyena and a man together

I

what?

like mixed their bodies together I mean

like if you cut them up and then smashed them together and then
sewed them back up

I don't know
what kind of a question is that

I bet a lot would happen

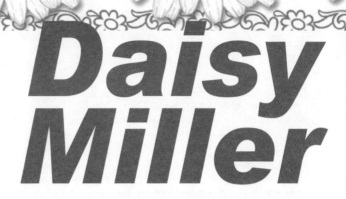

Daisy Miller

Part II

hi Daisy

hi

so I feel like I have to tell you something
normally I wouldn't say anything but I feel like
we're friends now

how kind of you

anyhow I just thought you should know
that there's someone in Vevey going around impersonating you
some sort of…coquette

coquette?

what I mean is
last night Mrs. Sanders saw someone dressed just like you
having dinner
in a restaurant

is that all?

a restaurant with MALE waiters

oh

naturally I told her it couldn't have been you
and that you'd sooner commit suicide
than eat dinner off a plate a male stranger had touched

that's very kind of you
but I'm afraid it must have been me she saw

oh

you know in New York we eat dinner from all kinds of waiters
all the time

oh my god
how fun for you
New York sounds just
it just sounds
talk later

bye then

byyyye

Les Misérables

where are you?

I am so there
this barricade is going to be an absolute HAPPENING you guys
don't start without me
i am on my way in like five minutes

Marius
I'm concerned that you don't really understand
the reason for our movement

oh my god
what do you mean

I sometimes question your commitment to the cause

how could you possibly even question that

I don't know, Marius
maybe it's because you have missed every one of
our clashes with the police
because you were still studying for the bar

to bring down the system from within!

Marius
your father is a baron
He's an actual baron

well
only a Napoleonic baron

that's still a baron

well when you say it like that

how did i say it

i don't know
it's just how you said it

■ ■ ■

are you coming or not?

i'm definitely so much coming for sure

quick question
can i bring my girlfriend

oh my god

she's totally into barricades
it'll be great
you'll love her
her dad was in jail so
she totally gets it if you know what i mean
like THE STRUGGLES
wait or he's a cop
I can't remember
he definitely has been to a jail
either as a cop or a jail guy
haha prisoner

"jail guy"
ANYHOW
on my way rn
oh hold up do you guys want me to bring anything??

Marius
could you
in your own words
explain what we are fighting for, do you think?
just as a favor to me

haha what a goofy question
ya goof
for the REVOLUTION

yes exactly
but could you list for me
one or two of the revolution's goals
or aims

to
rise up

right right
that is in a broad sense the goal of all revolutions
can you be even the slightest bit more specific

um
the right to work
no
the right to stop working
nobody has too many jobs
something about jobs
annnd voting??
it's the Huguenots
no
ugghh um um um
there's too much bread

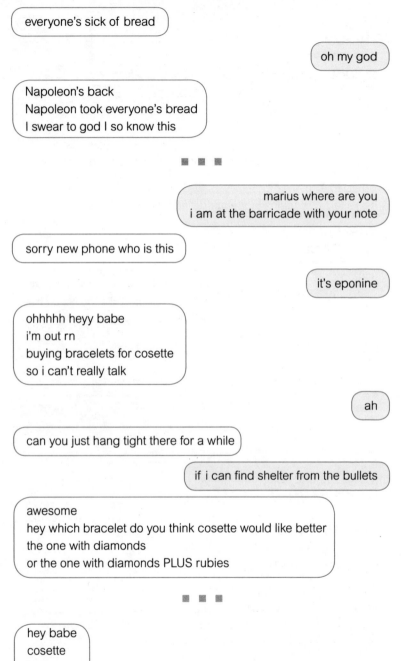

hi 😌

what does your dad do
like
for jail

what?

i mean like
your dad was in jail right
he's like a revolutionary or a murderer or something

no

shit
i guess that was someone else

someone else?

oh my god babe not like that
i just mean someone else's dad must have gone to jail

he did go to jail

oh right on
right on
that's right on for sure

but not for murder

oh awesome
my parents will be so relieved
Enjolras will be bummed though
oh babe while i have you
would you rather honeymoon on the Riviera
or just like, hot-air balloon around the world

I hadn't thought about it

should we make any decisions before the revolution?
mmm probably not
let's just say PROBABLY hot-air balloon around the world
but see what happens first
w/r/t revolutions
topple that damned Louis XVI!!!

that already happened

what

we already toppled Louis XVI
in the first revolution
in the 1700s

wait so do we not do a king anymore like at all

there's a different king now

what's his name

Louis-Philippe

oh my god how many guys named Louis are there
no wonder there's a revolution
OH
babe
do you want to come to the revolution with me??
it might be lame but we can bail whenever
and there's something going on after I know about
so we can just stop by
if we want

A Tale of Two Cities

Dr. Manette
They've taken him
they've taken him and I don't
know where he's gone

Taken whom, my dear

Charles
Charles, of course
He's in the Bastille
the things they're saying about him
they're terrible
what are we going to do, what will we do
we've got to save him

Don't you worry little one
I know just what to do
I'm going to make shoes

Rudyard Kipling

i'm bored
let's go shoot something

> okay
> What

i don't care
a tiger
or a Boer

> what was that last one?

I mean a bear

> oh
> Okay

haha must have been a weird typo
it's illegal to hunt men
but exhilarating

> what?

i said it was illegal
and also
execrable
execrable was the second word i said

Daisy Miller

Part III

Daisy
there's a castle just up the hill I want you to see
it's absolutely beautiful this time of year
please say you'll come
we'll walk the ramparts together and find lilac growing in the walls

oh how lovely
I'd be so pleased to come

oh my god
you were really going to do it
you were going to go to a castle alone with me

I don't understand

you wouldn't
you slut

Daisy Miller

Part IV

listen
Daisy
either run away with me this minute
or put on a goddamned shawl
you have the naked shoulders of a sultan's whore

The Sun Also Rises

> Brett
> Brett did you get that picture I sent you

> I did, yeah

> the picture of my penis I mean

> yes

> Brett
> guess how much of my penis I still have left
> you know
> after my accident
> after my penis accident

> I really don't want to play this game, Jake

> no come on guess

> I don't have unlimited texting
> these messages are kind of expensive for me

> I'll give you a hint:
> it's definitely SOME

■ ■ ■

at the bar
u coming
brett
brettttttttttttt
brettly
brettles

oh my god yes
give me ten minutes

okay
Awesome

I'm bringing Cohn with me

uuuuuuuuuuuuuuuuuuuuuuuuuuuuuuuuuuuuuuuuuuuuuuuuuuuugh

Jake

uuuuuuuuuuuuuughhhh

you don't own the bar
he can come to the bar if he wants to

no but brett
brett listen
fuck that guy

we'll be there in ten minutes

ask him if he wants to come with me to spain tomorrow

are you serious

uuuuuuuuuugh yes
i don't want to go to spain alone brett
that's so lame
who goes to spain by themsleves
haha
sleves

k fine i'll ask

see you soon
slevvvvves
hey im gonna send u a real quick pic of my penis

please don't

no its ok it'll be super quick

■ ■ ■

six missed calls

■ ■ ■

brett
brett did u get my messages
brett im so sorry
im so sorry we cant ever have sex
oh my god im so sorry
im gonna call you again just in case

■ ■ ■

its so awful that you cant have sex with me
im so sorry
thats why ur so lost brett
brett u cant keep living like this
going to bars and traveling
being friends with jewish guys
oh my god he's so jewish
and having sex with men who like you
its killing u brett
its killing u inside i can tell
hang on i gotta throw up im gonna call you
oh fuck im throwing up so bad
and we're all gonna die someday
and ur never even gonna have sex with me even

Agatha Christie

we've got to get off this train at once

my god
what's wrong?
has there been a murder?

not yet
but I believe they've let a JEW on board
tell that Arab boy to fetch our luggage at once

The Great Gatsby

> Niiiick
> Do you realize I never see you anymore
> I miss hanging out with you
> so much

> I miss you too Daisy

> Let's hang out RIGHT NOW

> Now?

> Now would be the best time!

It's awfully late

Let's just be spontaneous okay
Come pick me up and we'll do something wild

Where are you?

I would say definitely in the valley of ashes
nearrrrr the road
but not on it exactly

What are you doing there?

haha you are just
full of questions today

I'm just wondering why you want to hang out
all of a sudden
at midnight
in the valley of ashes
it feels like maybe all that you want is a ride

oh my god
how can you even say that
why are you so mean to me

Daisy Miller

Part V

have you seen Daisy today

I think she's out with that guy

what guy

the Italian one
you know
I can't remember the name

she has Italian friends?

yeah

ewwww

I know

never mind
forget I asked

uuuuugh

right

J. Alfred Prufrock

do you want to go out tonight

where

idk
like a one-night cheap hotel
or maybe one of those sawdust restaurants

Sawdust restaurants?
Like with the peanut shells on the floor?

with oyster shells

Oyster shells on the floor?

let's have a tedious argument in the streets

have you been drinking?

the sky is so beautiful tonight
like a patient etherized on a table

I'm coming over
I'm worried about you

there's yellow smoke on the window-panes

What kind of smoke?
Did you leave the stove on?

it's curling all around the house

You need to get out of the house

oh it's already sliding along the street

Get out of the house
now
I'm coming over

there will be time
there will be time for you and me

they say it I know they say it
they all say it

I honestly think you're being paranoid

"But his arms and legs are thin!"

Nobody says that about you

Or how thin my hair is getting

Your hair looks fine

You're all saying it
you think I can't understand you because you're talking
about Michelangelo
But I know what you're saying about me

I like the way your arms and legs look
I like your hair the way it is

You'd like me pinned and wriggling on the wall

I never said that
that's a terrible thing to say

I wish I were claws
I wish I were just a bunch of claws

like a crab?

no
just claws
ripping shit up with my claws
living underwater
can we go back to that oyster restaurant

that depends
are you going to pretend to be a pair of claws and scuttle around
in the lobster tank?

are you going to drive me there or what

■ ■ ■

S'io credesse che mia risposta fosse
A persona che mai tornasse al mondo,
Questa fiamma staria senza piu scosse

you know I don't speak Italian

Ma perciocche giammai di questo fondo

No idea what you're saying
so
let me know if you want to talk later in English

sorry new phone
who is this

■ ■ ■

I told you they hated me
I told you I could hear their voices dying with a dying fall

I don't think they hate you
I just think they were surprised to see you dressed like that

They've always hated me

I just don't think they were expecting you to come in shouting
"I am Lazarus, come from the dead, come back to tell you all"

well I'm sorry
I'm sorry I'm not Prince Hamlet or whatever
Sorry to be an easy tool

No one thinks you're a tool
It's just a weird thing to do at a dinner party

■ ■ ■

what are you doing
like right now

working

good good
that's good
do you think I should eat a peach

what
right now?

yeah

do you want to eat a peach?

idk
yeah

then you should eat a peach

yeah
could you give me a ride?

right now?

yeah

i'm at work

i know

where do you need a ride to?

the store

what store

i need a peach

can it wait?

not really
there's like
a bunch of mermaids here
and they definitely hate me

I don't know where that is

can we go back to that oyster restaurant
maybe they have peaches

I can't leave work to go buy you a peach right now

that's okay
that's fine
the mermaids keep singing about drowning me
but I'll probably be fine

okay
okay
tell me where you are and I'll come get you

awesome
and then we can go get peaches?

yes
we can go get peaches

okay

I'll be there in fifteen minutes

do you think I would look good with rolled trousers
like if I rolled up the cuffs
I think they would make my legs look less skinny

I don't know
Probably

actually
I don't know if I want a peach anymore

oh my god

buuutttt
you should still come get me
let's go out somewhere

Virginia Woolf

OH MY GOD MOM
WHAT DID I SAY I NEED TO WRITE FICTION
I NEEDED MONEY AND I NEED A ROOM OF MY OWN
NOT A ROOM YOU COME INTO WHEN I'M GONE AND CLEAN
UP
AND REARRANGE EVERYTHING AND GO THROUGH MY STUFF
THIS IS MY ROOM
STAY OUT
I KNOW YOU'VE BEEN READING MY JOURNALS
UNDER THE GUISE OF "TIDYING UP"
SO GUESS WHAT
MY FICTION IS THAT YOU'RE AN UTTER BITCH
TIDY THAT UP

William Faulkner

you know what would be nice

what

if you could just ravel out into time
that would be nice
it would be nice if you could just
ravel out into time

i guess that could be nice

but first you have to get ready to stay dead a long time

well

that's all that living is really

i guess technically

lets start now
ill go first
im a seed in the earth
you go next
(get ready to be dead)
(be a wet seed wild in the hot blind earth)

I
okay

youre not very good at this game

i guess not
sorry

its ok
my mother is a fish
and im a lot older than a lot of people who have died
and any live man is better than any dead man
but no live or dead man is much better than any other live
or dead man
so i understand

oh that's
that's good

■ ■ ■

hey i got you something

oh
you did?
Oh

i give you the mausoleum of all hope and desire

wow

not that you will remember time but that you might forget it
now and then

sure
sure
I can see how that would be a good thing

i knew youd like it :)

■ ■ ■

do you know what i hate

> no
> what do you hate

clocks

> oh
> how come

father said clocks slay time
time is dead as long as its being clicked off
by those little wheels
thats how they killed Christ you know

> little wheels?

yep
yep yep yep

■ ■ ■

i lost a cow once

> did you?

it was terrible
i loved that cow

> im sorry to hear that

it owed me forty years of back taxes too
if i ever find her i'll kill her

Daisy Miller

Part VI

look have you seen Daisy
I need to talk to her

oh my god
you haven't heard

heard what

that Daisy diiiied

what

yes

nooo

yesssss

oh my god
what happened

she went for a walk outside
with an Italian
at night
under the MOON

oh god of course

so
you know
obviously
that killed her

that'd kill anybody

i know
it especially killed her

Peter Pan

Hey

hey!

me and the guys are renting a yacht and heading to Croatia for this open-air festival
want to come??

oh are you guys still doing that?

well its not like a rental but we know a guy who says we can use his boat and he's super cool

when are you leaving?

mmm idk lemme check

okay

oh also
we don't have any sleeping space left on the yacht
but we're just gonna take peyote the whole way there so you won't even need a bed
just art
you know?

how long does it take to sail to Croatia

haha omg
holy shit
so i just talked to Dan and we're like
halfway there already i guess

you guys already left?

haha i know right
that's so fucked up
i don't even remember leaving
we're like
somewhere in the fucking ocean right now

wow

u should come over

come over to the ocean?

hell yes
hell yes come to the ocean
it's gonna be amazing
oh and when you come can you bring food and also money for food and also some money for tickets?
i didnt bring any of my stuff with me

where are you in the ocean?

ahh i gotta go they're opening the keg
see u sooooooon

■ ■ ■

ahh, Peter
Peter, my old friend Peter
you've come back to see me at last
I fear I have grown a great deal since the last time we met

oh ahhh sorry did i wake u up

I am a woman now, and an old woman at that

im literally not even here ok
i just like
you said to come by if i ever needed anything
and i just needed to borrow some money for a thing

Well, of course, Peter
anything you need
I'll get my pocketbook

oh no dont worry i already
its fine ive got what i need

come into the drawing room and talk with me a while, Peter

um
is your skin still doing that folding thing

I am old
I have wrinkles now

yeah haha
ew
to be super honest hospitals freak me out

so i don't think i can stay real long

it's not a hospital, Peter
I am old but I am not dying

right right
well
i can't come in the house cos i haven't been invited

Oh

ahh sorry but thats like how my powers work

Is that not true of vampires?

well yeah
vampires and me too

I invite you in, Peter
I invite you
Come sit with me and talk a while

ahhh sorry new phone who is this

The Great Gatsby

Part II

Hi Nick 😊

Daisy
what time is it?

mmm
Late

where are you?

You
You are going to laugh at this

am I really

well obviously not if you choose to be a dick about it

you probably won't laugh then
but I can't help that

what do you want

i need a ride 😃

where are you

remember that valley with ashes in it

I remember

basically just there

I'm leaving now

oh also
you should call the police
somebody's dead here

somebody's dead?
who's dead?
dead from what?

oh i don't know
we weren't close or anything
looks like they've been hit by a car

would that be your car, do you think?

can't say
hard to tell
definitely A car, though
tell you what
you just come out here and get me
and somebody else can call the police

Part IV

Sweet Valley High

Jess are you there?

yeah I'm here

Where were you?

what do you mean

Did you not get any of my texts?

no

The Sweet Sixteen people were here
for the interview about the fundraiser

they already came?

you weren't here
so I tried to do the best I could without you
Oh I know I was awful

I'm sure they won't print anything I said
I'm so sorry you couldn't make it

hey Liz

Yeah?

do you ever catch anything
when you're fishing
for compliments

■ ■ ■

oh my god
oh my god they're not moving, Jess
I think they're both dead
Jesus Christ God
they're dead, they're dead
the car flipped and nobody's moving
oh my god

well
you wouldn't spike the punch like I asked!!
so I had to spike it myself

WHAT DID YOU PUT IN IT

ohhh my godddd i don't KNOW
something from a jar??
haha i mean booze obviously
booze from a jar
but i don't knooooww
that's why I asked you to do it

I would never have helped you if I knew you were going to do
something like this

then I guess you don't have what it takes to be
Jungle Prom Queen
which
is that the same thing as regular prom queen?
haha what kind of school has two proms
anyhow I thought Bruce looked crazy hot tonight
do you think he has a date for the next prom?

Bruce is dead
they're all dead

yeah he didn't look that good tonight I guess

■ ■ ■

Oh, Jess
I hate New York sometimes
I miss Sweet Valley so much

oh my god I know
they don't even have a Dairi Burger there!!!
what kind of a city

It's just so empty
Like this morning at the coffee shop
I really felt like the interaction I had with the waitress
when I asked if they had any stevia
lacked authenticity
I sure wish this news internship were over already
but who knows when they'll be done having news here

haha remember Mom

I knew you'd understand, anyhow

remember Dad
what happened to them
where do they go all the time

■ ■ ■

Jess
Jess where are you

haha what

the pep rally is in a few minutes and we need you for the pyramid

oh that
something tells me we're not going to be cheering much tonight

what do you mean

let's just say
we won't have to worry about those jerks at Big Mesa anymore

Jessica what did you do?

let's just say their plans to trash
the field after the big game have
"gone up in smoke"

Jessica
what did you do

let's just say their "gym"
is "on fire"
with SVH spirit
hey do you want to go to the Dairi Burger?
I'm all hungry
and covered in ash

The Outsiders

no you're right

■ ■ ■

man you know who i hate

who

guys with green eyes
or i guess
MOST guys with green eyes
would you say my eyes are greenish-gray, or grayish-green

i don't know

your eyes are icy blue, so they're always icy blue
but sometimes my eyes are more greenish-gray than
grayish-green
which i think is better

huh

hey do you want to come over and watch the sunset

yeah okay
i guess so

okay great
i mean it's the same sunset as the one at your house
so don't expect anything big

i won't

i really think they're more grayish-green right now than
anything else

yeah maybe

not green like Darry's anyhow
they're green like ice, but bluer than that
I really need to update my eye color journal

your what?

see you soon for the sunset!!!

■ ■ ■

so what did you think

what did i think of what

what did you think of all the drawings of Dally i sent you

oh yeah

do you think he'll like them?
do you think they're any good

there sure are
a lot of them

do you think i made his eyes look enough like blue ice
that was really what i was going for
because his eyes look like blazing blue ice

i definitely think you did

oh good
i was kind of worried
that they didn't look enough like blue ice that's blazing

no, they're–
you did a really good job
they're really nice

well i wanted to do something special for his birthday
and it was either this or a switchblade
and i figured everyone else was already getting him a switchblade

right

what's a guy gonna do with six switchblades, you know?

yeah

such a thing as too many switchblades
anyhow i'm glad you think they're good

yeah

you want one?

oh
i think i'm okay

i can draw you one real fast
it won't take two minutes

no i'm okay

i'll draw you one just in case
his eyes look like blue ice
blue ice!

■ ■ ■

you awake?

yeah
what's wrong?

i had that dream again

oh

that dream where i got the haircut
that was the worst day of my life, the day Johnny cut my hair
remember?

yeah i remember

if a guy doesn't have his silky reddish-blonde hair
that's just a little redder than Soda's and swirls just right
well what kind of a guy is he?

i don't know

plus it was real sad when Johnny died, too

yeah

died before his hair could even grow back

i remember

his hair looked terrible when he died
i was embarrassed to even go to the funeral

yeah me too

The American Girl Series

nellie
nellie why didnt u come to the hedge today
to the lessons hedge)for lessons)

> I'm sorry, Miss Parkington
> I wasn't able to get away in time and

i was going to teach you more lessons
is this about my birthday party
are u mad at me

> no Samantha…

because i told you
its not that youre not my friend
you are my friend

> I'm glad to be your friend

u are just more of my FACTORY friend
and not really
my "birthday party" friend

> I understand
> I couldn't get away from the mill

that's all

guess how many kinds of ice cream we had

I don't know

haha there are only three kinds of ice cream nellie
everyone knows that

I see

youve got a lot of lessons ahead of you nellie
ICE CREAM LESSONS
only we're out of ice cream right now
because we ate so much
(at my birthday party)

■ ■ ■

Miss Felicity -
I must thank you for coming by last week to my hiding-place
the biscuits and canteen you brought were sorely needed
I know once I can enlist with the Patriots
I will be a burden to you no longer
I fear that before that day, however
I must trespass on your kindness one last time
and ask when you will return
as the water you so kindly brought me
ran out several days ago
and I am afraid to venture forth in daylight
and this fetid swamp provides me with no relief

BEN
BEN I'M GETTING A PONY

I congratulate you, Miss Felicity
that is wonderful news

Perhaps
perhaps it shall make the trip shorter
when you do come again

I will name her Penny!!!

for I have grown weak from thirst

She is the color of a penny
is why I have chosen that name, Ben

A good name, that
I trust I can keep my strength up
long enough to see her myself

I am going to brush her mane EVERY DAY

■ ■ ■

Harriet

Addy.

Mother wanted me to ask you
if you'd like to go to the fair tomorrow with us

Did she now

since we'll be working at the same booth together
all afternoon
Father's offered to give us a ride in his wagon

oh, his milk wagon?

yes
his milk wagon
He only has the one wagon
you know that

Like father like daughter I suppose
he only has one wagon
and you only have one dress

You can just say no, Harriet
if you don't want to come with us
you can just say no

Addy
do you even know how many dresses I have

I'm sorry if I insulted you with my invitation
you don't have to come

Addy
I have SEVEN dresses
I have a dress for every day of the week
I have a dress for Monday

look
forget I said anything
I'll see you tomorrow

I have a dress for Tuesday
on Wednesday I have a different dress

and on Thursday you have a fourth
I get it

do you though

I think I grasp the prinsiple of the thing

oh my God
Addy Walker

how DO you spell principle, Harriet?
is it with an S?
or a C?

you are going to be so sorry that you ever

Maybe we should ask a spelling expert
Maybe we should ask someone who won

that you EVER

a spelling
medal
for spelling the word principle correctly
I only have the one dress
which I pinned the spelling medal on
so you can see the medal every day

The Baby-Sitters Club

Hey Claudia
I know math is really tough for you
but even you should know
that two dollars an hour
for six hours
means we're at least twelve dollars short
of what should be in the treasury

> i know how much twelve is, Kristy
> and i didn't take your stupid money

look
all I'm saying
is that someone that good at hiding candy in her room
probably has a few great places to hide twelve dollars
like maybe in an incredibly ugly macrame wallet with velvet
appliqués

yeah well
at least my dad still lives at home
unlike some people's dads
unlike your dad

■ ■ ■

Kristy
Kristy? It's Mallory
I hope you don't mind my texting you
I had to get your number from Mary Anne
but she's not around or something
I guess
I was just wondering if we had a meeting today?
I'll check with Stacey

■ ■ ■

Kristy, Mrs. Dawes said that you never showed up on Friday
to babysit the girls
She had to cancel her plans
she's really upset
What's going on with you lately?

oh sorry
i probably just couldn't hear the phone ring when she called
this mansion is sooooo big
Watson's mansion i mean

I know which mansion you mean

my new dad Watson
who does live with us
Claaaaaudia

Claudia's not here

i know
i know that

■ ■ ■

Hey Stacey!
It's Mallory
do you know if we're meeting today?
I heard Dawn mention something about it
but for some reason I can't get a hold of anybody
let me know if this is the right number for you
might be an old number
I made brownie bars so I hope it's today haha
i mean any time we meet is fine
it's all fine with me
oh my god and the brownies have sugar in them
I swear to God I wasn't thinking
I'm really sorry, Stacey

■ ■ ■

shit
shit
claudia have you seen karen

not lately

i can't find her
like she's not in the house

last i saw her
she was borrowing your glue gun to put rhinestones on her
homework like i told her an hour ago

well what have you been doing for the last hour then

i was enamelling

what have YOU been doing for the last hour Stacey

you know i don't like you guys to watch me take my insulin shots

oh
i didn't know that's what we were calling robbie brewster now

CLAUDIA
i cannot believe you
oh my god
by the way did you give mallory my real phone number?
because that is not okay
i got like
thirty texts from her this morning

Nancy Drew

Nancy? Are you coming?
I've been waiting by the old oak in the park for almost an hour
I tried calling your father and he said you went out to the lake
with Bess and George
but Bess came back ages ago
I guess maybe you didn't take your phone with you
anyhow the picnic is here
and I am here too
whenever you get here
no rush!
I miss you

oh Ned
I'm so sorry
but I am so close to figuring out who the jewel thieves are
I think it has something to do with the ghostly figure that
frightened Ms. Martin after the gala
and the twins are pretty sure they saw something out
on the island

what did they see?

oh
could be anything
jewels
or anything
anyhow so it's really important that I go sailing with them

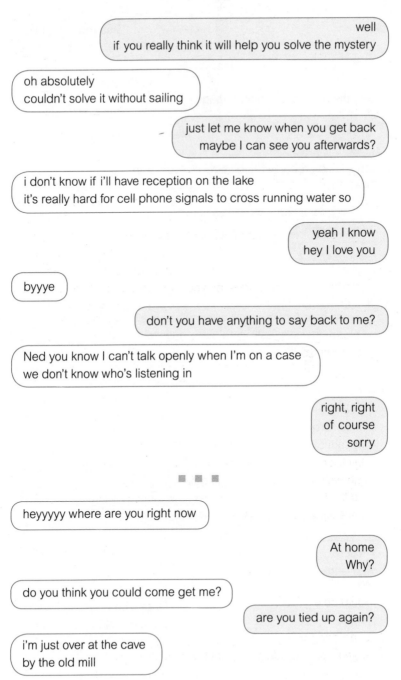

well
if you really think it will help you solve the mystery

oh absolutely
couldn't solve it without sailing

just let me know when you get back
maybe I can see you afterwards?

i don't know if i'll have reception on the lake
it's really hard for cell phone signals to cross running water so

yeah I know
hey I love you

byyye

don't you have anything to say back to me?

Ned you know I can't talk openly when I'm on a case
we don't know who's listening in

right, right
of course
sorry

heyyyyy where are you right now

At home
Why?

do you think you could come get me?

are you tied up again?

i'm just over at the cave
by the old mill

so you're tied up
in a cave

you know
near the burned-down orphanage

please just answer the question

you should probably bring some scissors with you

for the rope?

there appears to be some rope here, yes

are you tied up with it?

Ned look
it's really hard for me to text with my hands all tied up like this
so please just stop asking so many questions and
get over here ok

■ ■ ■

Nancy!
Nancy I can see that's you
it's me
Ned
I'm on the other side of the baccarat table

You don't have to let on that you know me if you're working

I'm sorry
who is this?

Nancy, I can see that it's you
You're just wearing bangs

Please leave me alone
I am a troubled heiress who wants only to play baccarat
and forget her troubles

are you in disguise?

My only disguise are my troubles
is my troubles
Please excuse the English

who's that man you're with?

I'm sorry I wanted to follow the kidnappers into the cave, Ned

That's all right

I really am sorry though

I know

I'm sorry we got tied up again

It's okay

I'm can't believe what they did to your face
I had no idea they were so desperate

I know

I really don't know how we're going to get out of this one

Me neither

this is worse than when we found out it was George who murdered Bess

God

remember that?

yeah I remember

that was horrible

it really was

Atlas Shrugged

happy birthday

Oh, Dag
you remembered

I got you something

you did?
that's so sweet

I got you the greatest gift one human being can offer
another person

you didn't have to do that
what is it?

I have achieved something

Oh, gosh

well I made an achievement all by myself and no one can
touch it or sully it with their dirty jealous fingers
and no one can take it away from me
never never never
so
happy birthday

thank you, Dagny

Yes.
You're welcome.

COMMUNISM

what about Communism?

WATCH OUT FOR IT

IT'S EVERYWHERE

SO WATCH OUT

all right

all right

I will.

■ ■ ■

do you love me, Hank
really love me, I mean?
I love you, you know
I love the way you run the motor of the world
I love you like a train

Like a what?

it's the highest and purest form of love there is, Hank
the love of a woman for a train
gosh but I love trains
that little whistle
the knowledge that you could roll merrily over any one of your
enemies and crush their thick skulls with your harnessed steel-
beasts
those hot little rolls they have in the dining car
do we have any of those rolls left?

I'll find out

trains trains trains
I do love em

■ ■ ■

do you know who I just hate

who?

everybody
everybody but us

■ ■ ■

do you want to come over

right now?

yeah

you know what we should do?

all right

what?

you should just
stay over
and we can go on strike

on strike from what?

on strike from everybody
because fuck em

■ ■ ■

I don't know if you noticed this
but my shoulder was naked in my evening gown tonight

I did see that

it was my gown's only ornament, that naked shoulder

Very nice

well, also the diamond band
that was the other ornament I had on
so the shoulder was naked
but my wrist had diamonds on it

Right

did those diamonds make you think of chains
Chains are so terribly feminine, you know
almost as feminine as a naked shoulder

mm

Guess what
my shoulder is naked right now

Oh

well
underneath my blazer it is naked
both of my shoulders are naked
underneath my blazer

I see

does that make you want to chain them up

I'm awfully sorry
but I have to go to a meeting now

you can chain me up after your meeting then

I'll think about that

■ ■ ■

Francisco
Francisco are you awake?
Francisco?

what is it

Francisco, I can't sleep

I'm sorry

I had a bad dream

the one about the Communists?

I don't want to talk about it
tell me about the root of money again, Francisco

what time is it?

Come on, Francisco
tell me
I'll help get you started
"Money is a root of exchange…"

Dag, please

I have to work in the morning

"Paper is a mortgage on wealth that does not exist…"

you don't even need me to tell you what money is

I like the way that you tell it best

all rightt
all right, I'll tell you about the root of money

do that voice you do for the looters, ok
do your looters voice

I'll do my looters voice

k

Fight Club

hey have you seen my work khakis?
I think I might have lost them or something
which is crazy because I had them on yesterday
have you seen them?

its only after we've lost everything
that we're free to do anything

ok yes definitely

you have to lose everything
everything includes pants
pants are a thing, so

no yes
I am super on board with that

like a noun or whatever, pants are

I'm just wondering
specifically
where my pants are
because they are my actual last pair of pants

YOU ARE NOT YOUR PANTS

I know

I AM NOT YOUR PANTS

no I definitely know that
I just need these pants for work

YOU ARE NOT YOUR JOB

I'm not trying to be my job I swear
but we are down to our last forty bucks
I really
we can't afford to lose this money right now

you are not special

what?

you're not a fucking snowflake

I know that
I don't think it's being a snowflake to want pants

everything is decaying
we're all just part of the same compost heap
your pants are decaying

my pants are in the compost heap?

well everything is in the compost heap
so you do the fucking math
you do the compost math

■ ■ ■

fuck the fridge is out again
do you mind calling Jasper sometime today
let him know we need to make an appointment

did you ever think that maybe
your life is just too complete?

is the fridge too complete?

you have to break everything
to make something better

i really don't think your malaise is the fridge's fault

it isn't not the fridge's fault
only after disaster can we be resurrected
and breaking the fridge

that's part of your resurrection

our resurrection
we've all been raised on TV to believe
that one day we'd all be millionaires

> huh
> what show was that

and movie gods

> I mostly watched scooby doo
> I think

and rock stars

> gilligan's island maybe
> whatever that show was that was like
> it wasn't the smurfs
> but it kind of was the smurfs
> but underwater?
> they had weird spout noses i remember

but we won't
and we're slowly learning that fact
and we're very, very pissed off

> and this is the fridge's fault

is your life really so empty
that you honestly can't think of a better way
to spend these moments

> god
> okay fine
> i'll call jasper
> you won't have to do anything

ive been peeing in your soup
like every day

> what?

nothing
fuck you
fuck the fridge
do you own your fridge
or does your fridge own you

it's not even my fridge
you had this fridge when I moved in

i was wrong about you, man
you really are your pants

■ ■ ■

ugh
do you know what's the worst

what?

moms
fucking moms
and like
IKEA
and our jobs
because they trap us in nests
god i hate how easy it is
to just get jobs
and make money all the time
and have a mom
it's not real, you know?

right

like "oh i'm your mom"
"i'm gonna love you and raise you and shit"
well guess what mom
i'm gonna set skyscrapers on fire
because god's not my dad

what?

i'm gonna shit on the mona lisa
and beat up beautiful guys
because of consumerism

huh

shit right on the mona lisa

■ ■ ■

heyyyy
u comin to fight club tonight
gonna be super fighty
hey
hey are u around
i need a ride
to fight club
(so i can fight)
DUDE ANSWER ME
ARE YOU COMING
OR ARE YOU NOT COMING
TO FIGHT CLUB
TO THE FIGHT CLUB THAT YOU FUCKING HELPED ME INVENT
I SWEAR TO GOD I WILL PISS ON YOUR NEW PANTS
IF YOU DO NOT ANSWER ME
IN THE NEXT FIVE FUCKING DAMN ASS SECONDS

> jesus
> yes
> i'm coming to fight club

OH MY GOD

WHAT IS LITERALLY THE FIRST RULE

> what?

> jesus
> Tyler

LITERALLY THE FIRST RULE WE MADE FOR FIGHT CLUB

> please don't piss on my pants

THE ONE RULE

> you're talking about it
> you're calling it fight club right now
> how is that not the same thing

"HOW IS THAT NOT THE SAME THING"
enjoy your piss pants

The Lorax

THAT'S COMPOSTABLE YOU KNOW

I'm sorry?

POST-IT NOTES ARE ACTUALLY COMPOSTABLE
SO YOU SHOULDN'T THROW THEM OUT

Who is this?

I AM THE LORAX

the what

I SPEAK FOR THE TREES

okay well
thanks for the advice

DID YOU KNOW YOU CAN ALSO COMPOST YOUR OWN HAIR

I didn't know that

YOU CAN
SO ARE YOU GOING TO TAKE
THOSE POST-ITS OUT OF
THE TRASH THEN

■ ■ ■

DID YOU GET THAT EMAIL I FORWARDED YOU
ABOUT THE DANGERS OF E-CIGARETTES

What email?

CHECK YOUR SPAM FOLDER
SOMETIMES MY EMAILS GET STUCK IN SPAM FOLDERS

I thought you spoke for the trees

I SPEAK FOR A LOT OF THINGS

■ ■ ■

DO YOU HAVE ANY IDEA
HOW MANY TAMPONS THE AVERAGE WOMAN USES IN A YEAR

I'm in class right now
I can't talk about tampons

TAMPONS CAN'T EVER TALK
THEY DON'T HAVE MOUTHS
THAT'S WHY I SPEAK FOR THEM

okay

ENOUGH TAMPONS TO MAKE A TRUFFULA TREE
THAT'S HOW MANY
HAVE YOU CONSIDERED THE DIVA CUP

That's really personal, Lorax

NOTHING IS PERSONAL WHEN YOU SPEAK FOR THE TREES

and tampons?

AND ALSO TAMPONS AND SOMETIMES E-CIGARETTES YES

I'll think about it

THERE'S ONE IN YOUR PURSE IF YOU CHANGE YOUR MIND
JUST IN CASE YOU NEED ONE TODAY

You put one in my purse?
You went through my purse?

OH YOU MEAN YOUR LEATHER PURSE
YOUR PURSE MADE OUT OF DEAD SKIN

this is too weird
I'm throwing it out

DON'T

don't what?

DON'T REACH IN YOUR PURSE

Lorax if I reach in my purse what will I find in there

DID YOU KNOW THAT YOU CAN MAKE YOUR OWN SOAP OUT
OF DISCARDED COCA COLA SYRUP
WHICH MOST RESTAURANTS WILL GIVE TO YOU FOR FREE IF
YOU ASK NICELY

Lorax are you in my purse right now

YES

Why

I FELL ASLEEP WHEN I WAS PUTTING THE DIVA CUP IN THERE
YOUR PURSE IS REALLY SOFT

oh wow
are you okay?

NOT REALLY
LEATHER IS REALLY SOFT
I DIDN'T REALIZE HOW SOFT IT IS

I'm sorry I made you touch leather

SOMETIMES I GET SLEEPY SPEAKING FOR THINGS
IT WAS JUST SO SOFT AND I WAS SO SLEEPY

Do you want me to let you stay in the purse for the rest of the day

YES PLEASE
I WOULD LIKE THAT VERY MUCH

Okay

CAN WE PLANT A TREE LATER THOUGH
I MEAN IF YOU HAVE TIME
JUST ONE TREE ON THE WAY HOME

Maybe

OKAY
BECAUSE I THINK MAYBE SOME OF MY FRIENDS WILL
COME BACK
IF WE DO THAT

Maybe they willl

JUST HOPE SOME OF MY FRIENDS COME BACK

I know

YOU'RE MY FRIEND NOW TOO THOUGH

I know

SO I GUESS IT'S WORKING ALREADY

I guess so

MUST BE ALL THOSE POST ITS WE COMPOSTED THIS
MORNING

Go back to sleep

OKAY THANK YOU

Rebecca

oh Mrs. de Winter
I realized after I took you on a tour of the master wing
I forgot to tell you about her clothes

whose clothes?

Whose clothes do you think

Rebecca's?

of course
they were incredible
even her taste in nightgowns was impeccable
not like some nightgowns i could name
not like some nightgowns I have to regularly launder
and fold and put away

I see

your nightgowns, specifically
I hate your nightgowns
so if when you come home tonight
you see a lot of R's scribbled in lipstick
and also blood all over your nightgowns
that was me

Ah

in case you wondered
who that was

Well, now I won't wonder

the R is for Rebecca

I see

also I can't stand the kind of tea you buy
so I ripped open all the bags
and strewed the leaves throughout the great hallway

oh dear

because honestly
BAGGED tea?
this is a stately home
like OF ENGLAND
this house has an actual name
you don't even have a name
literally no one has ever mentioned your name
it's just "where is my wife" and "this is Mrs. De Winter"
"the second" Mrs. De Winter
"the lesser" Mrs. De Winter
"the Mrs. De Winter who gets her tea in bags"
god i hate you
so much

■ ■ ■

you're using the wrong fork you know

Please
Please, I'm trying to have dinner with my husband
and I'd like to be left alone

you'll never be alone
not here
not in Manderley
her spirit's in the very floors and walls
in the mirrors
in the rooms behind the doors you'll never open
in the fork you're not using properly

Where are you?
I can't see you anywhere

that doesn't surprise me
not at all
Rebecca would have spotted me in a second

I'm sure I'm very sorry
but I can't see you and I'm not Rebecca

like I didn't already know that

■ ■ ■

I couldn't help but notice that you didn't jump out your
window last night
even after I left it open for you

No, I didn't

you know who would have jumped out the window
if I'd asked her to?

PLEASE STOP

I'll give you a hint
you have the same last name
and married the same man
also one of you is dead and one of you is not

It's Rebecca
Rebecca, I know it's her
I know it's Rebecca, I KNOW IT'S HER

■ ■ ■

oh my God
that is your SALAD fork
this is the fish course
what is wrong with you

Cormac McCarthy

just got here
saving you a table
hey
you on your way?
hey
are you coming?

You forget what you want to remember
and you remember what you want to forget

look
it's fine if you can't make it
it's just people are starting to head home
but if you're on your way

Nobody wants to be here and nobody wants to leave

oh
um
okay
I just thought you said you were going to try to make it
that's all
it's fine
I'll have another birthday next year so it's no big deal

yesterday is all that does count
What else is there?
Your life is made out of the days it's made out of
Nothin else

okay well
Thanks
Whatever in creation exists without my knowledge exists without my consent
oh
you tell em that
tell who?
tell em
tell everything that exists that i don't know about yet
it's not allowed
i don't know if that's
i don't know if i can do that
There is no forgiveness for women.
A man may lose his honor and regain it again.
But a woman cannot. She cannot.

well
you know

real shame, that

■ ■ ■

what's the most you ever lost on a coin toss

i dunno
five bucks maybe
why

no reason

■ ■ ■

is the fire real

is what fire real

is the fire real?
are you carrying it?

what fire are you talking about

the fire inside you

where is the fire

oh it's just a little fire
kept it small
kept it hidden
you know what

what

the freedom of birds is an insult to me

where are you going

you know where

please don't do anything to birds
I'm coming over

Carry the fire

WHAT FIRE

you'll see

The Hunger Games
I told you what I was gonna name my bakery
if we ever get out of here
right?
Peeta I'm actually really tired
I'm gonna name it The Hunger Grains
I'm going to go to sleep now, Peeta
It's a play on "The Hunger Games"
because it's something everyone already knows
but with a little twist
you should go to sleep too.
Only no one will be hungry at The Hunger Grains
well
maybe at first
when they get there
but not once they've had my Ruebarb pie
oh my God

hey Katniss

Peeta I cannot talk right now

oh
im sorry

remember how we talked about this?

i dunno

remember how we talked about how I can't talk when I'm hunting?
because of what else I need my hands for?

because you need your hands for holding arrows

Because I need my hands for holding arrows.

yeah i remember

so that's why I said
don't try to get in touch with me
unless you're having an emergency

yeah

are you having an emergency?

definitely

is it a real emergency?
or is it a f...

it's a frosting emergency

Peeta
a frosting emergency isn't the same thing as a real emergency

it is to me
it is to this cake and also it is to me

I'm turning my phone off

frosting emergencies are just as real as other kinds of
emergencies

William
Carlos
Williams

i have eaten everything
that was in the icebox
you should probably go to the store again.
-wcw

■ ■ ■

i have eaten the little red wheelbarrow
that was in the icebox
and upon which so much depended
forgive me
i don't even know why i did that
i guess i thought it was one of those little ice cream cakes
you know the kind that they shape to look like cars or whatever
that shit was disgusting
hey do we have any ice cream cakes though
-wcw

■ ■ ■

i have eaten the emperor of ice cream
who thought he could hide from me in the icebox
Let be be his finale of seem
sorry
-wcw

■ ■ ■

hi babe
are you at the store?
hi babe there's something weird going on with the dishwasher
it won't close all the way
i think one of the big wooden spoons fell through the slats or
something
it keeps making this weird ca-chunk ca-chunk sound
i'll call you and leave a message
so you can hear what it sounds like
-wcw

■ ■ ■

3 missed calls
1 new voicemail

■ ■ ■

hey if you're at the store
would you pick me up some more of that red thing i like
in the tall box

honey i'm not at the store right now
i'm already on my way home
can you pick it up yourself this afternoon?

You sullen pig of a woman
you force me into the mud
with your stinking ash-cart

honey i'm sorry but i was just at the store this morning
and i'm exhausted and i'm almost home

Well–
all things turn bitter in the end
whether you choose the right or
the left way

fine
fine i'll go to the store

mm also we are out of plums again
so can you pick up some more while you're there
thank youuuuuuuuuuuuu babe
-wcw

Harry Potter

I'm serious, Ron

lolll no
there's no way a "higgs boson" is a real thing

It is real!
It's very important
It's an elementary particle

what does it do then

Well
it's a particle
and it sort of involves multiple identical particles
to exist in the same state and place

like magic

No, not like magic
not like magic at all
like science

haha what is science though

Ron.

im serious

i don't know what it is
also what is math
i keep hearing about it
but no one can explain what it is to me

Math is a field of study
It's short for mathematics
It's concerned with quantity and structure and space

hermione I dont even know how to tip at a restaurant
i dont even know how to do percentals

Percentages

i dont know that either

Oh, Ron.

also whats a credit card
because i keep getting offers for them in the mail
are they magic too?

No
No, honey, credit cards aren't magic

because ive signed up for six or nine of them
does six come before or after nine

Ron you haven't used them yet have you

all you have to do is give the card to a shopkeep
and they swipe it over a little machine
and then they give you things
it's wicked

Ron
promise me you won't use your credit cards again

well I won't
but I gave some of them to this Nigerian man
or gave the numbers of them to him
the other day
so he might use them, I dunno

you did what

he's a prince, Hermione!
a real prince
well
he was a prince
he's in a little trouble right now
but I fixed it with a few of my credit cards
so he's all right now

Oh, my God

i thought youd be proud of me 😊

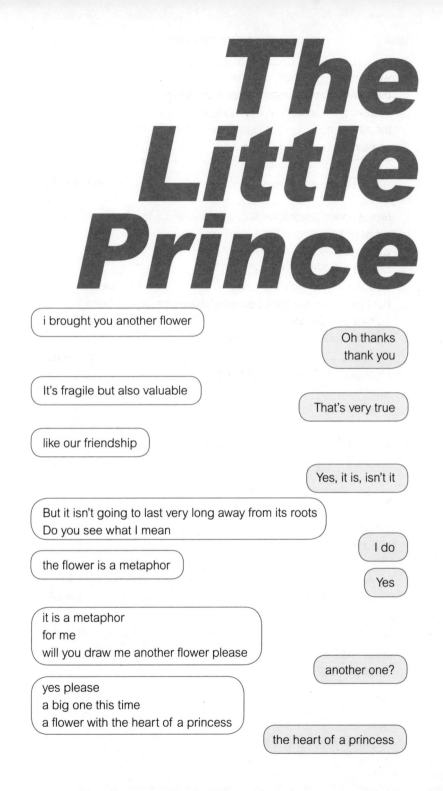

yes but you mustn't draw the princess
i must only be able to sense her in the drawing of the flower

what happened to the last flower i drew for you

a fox took it

a fox?

yes
a fox in a wooden top hat and a greatcoat made of whist came by
and asked if he could have it
he said it cured his arthritis

if i draw you another flower
do you think you will be able to hang onto it?

i cannot predict what a fox will need

no right of course
well if i draw you another flower
will you at least tell me where you've been sleeping and showering
and getting food?
because my plane is still nowhere near fixed and i'm almost out of
water

now you are speaking like a grownup again
now when i look at my flower all i will think of is your greed
your lust for money
your inability to see true beauty

i'm just so thirsty all the time
you know my plane was shot down because I was in the war
right?
I was in a war

i must go now

please
just tell me where you're getting water

my planet needs me